how2become

Pass the Professional Skills Tests for Initial Teacher Training (ITT)

www.How2Become.com

As part of this product you have also received FREE access to online tests that will help you to pass the professional skills tests.

To gain access, simply go to:

www.PsychometricTestsOnline.co.uk

Get more products for passing any test at:

www.How2Become.com

Orders: Please contact How2Become Ltd, Suite 14, 50 Churchill Square Business Centre, Kings Hill, Kent ME19 4YU.

You can order through Amazon.co.uk under ISBN: 9781911259060, via the website www.How2Become.com or through Gardners.com.

ISBN: 9781911259060

First published in 2016 by How2Become Ltd.

Typeset for How2Become Ltd by Anton Pshinka.

Disclaimer

Every effort has been made to ensure that the information contained within this guide is accurate at the time of publication. How2Become Ltd is not responsible for anyone failing any part of any selection process as a result of the information contained within this guide. How2Become Ltd and their authors cannot accept any responsibility for any errors or omissions within this guide, however caused. No responsibility for loss or damage occasioned by any person acting, or refraining from action, as a result of the material in this publication can be accepted by How2Become Ltd.

The information within this guide does not represent the views of any third party service or organisation.

CONTENTS

Introduction 7

The QTS Literacy Skills Test **13**

Spelling 17

Punctuation 45

Grammar 69

Comprehension 115

Mock Test 139

Answers And Explanations 155

The QTS Numeracy Skills Test **167**

General Skills 171

Mental Arithmetic 179

Written Arithmetic 193

Mock Test 225

Answers And Explanations 237

Initial Teacher Training **247**

A Few Final Words 261

Glossary 263

INTRODUCTION

Becoming a teacher is no simple task. It requires commitment and hard work, as well as a number of specific qualifications. In particular, you need to obtain Qualified Teacher Status (QTS) in order to teach in England and Wales. This applies to any kind of teaching, whether it be primary or secondary, English or maths, music or history.

In order to obtain QTS, you must first pass two skills tests – one for literacy and one for numeracy. These skills tests are meant to ensure that trainee teachers have literacy and numeracy skills which meet the requirements of a teacher in the UK. At first, it may seem unusual to be tested on literacy and numeracy skills if you have no intention of becoming an English or maths teacher. However, there are several reasons for why a strong understanding of both literacy and numeracy is required:

- One of these is that almost all specialisms and subjects in teaching rest on a foundation of either literacy, numeracy, or both.

- Secondly, there's a lot to teaching outside of the classroom. As a teacher, you may be required to proofread a colleague's work, create a report which may involve some maths, or read and gain an understanding of government documents which may be important to teaching.

Who takes the QTS skills tests?

Regardless of your background, your literacy and numeracy skills will need to be tested before becoming a teacher in England or Wales. The QTS skills tests are not taken in Scotland or Northern Ireland, but if you train in these countries, you will need to apply for QTS status in order to teach in England or Wales. In addition, QTS only applies for the country in which it was awarded. So, if you take and pass the QTS skills tests in Wales, your QTS only applies in Wales. However, it isn't particularly difficult for teachers to apply for QTS in the other country (either England or Wales, depending on where you applied initially).

If you have teaching qualifications outside of the UK, you will still need to apply for QTS in order to become a teacher in England and Wales. However, if you've already become a teacher in another country and have a decent grasp of the English language, you will be in a good position to take the QTS skills tests. Regardless of your background and entry into teaching, the kind of QTS skills test you take will be the same, and therefore the contents of this book will apply to you.

What do the QTS skills tests consist of?

As previously mentioned, there are two skills tests which must be passed before QTS is awarded.

The literacy skills test focuses on four main areas:

- Spelling
- Punctuation
- Grammar
- Comprehension

The numeracy skills test contains questions which cover a range of mathematical skills which you may find useful in your day-to-day life:

- Conversions
- Measurements
- Fractions
- Percentages

Moreover, you will be tested on less common mathematical areas such as averages.

One vital thing to note is that the QTS skills tests do not assess your teaching skills. Instead, they are used to ensure that you have the required understanding of literacy and numeracy in order to teach effectively. So, while the QTS skills tests aren't a measurement of your ability to teach, they are important to determine whether or not you would make a good teacher. Thus, you must take the tests seriously if you wish to obtain a teaching career.

Most of the material that you will face in the QTS skills tests will be quite familiar. You've probably had to calculate the time in the past, or determine the average from a series of numbers. While you might not have had to spot the punctuation errors in a text, you have probably been exposed to enough material to be able to spot mistakes in a piece of writing. However, there is still much that you will need to prepare for.

How can I prepare for the test?

The best way to prepare for the QTS skills tests is to make use of the resources in this book. Each section will provide you with explanations for different devices and challenges that you might face in the QTS skills tests, as well as practice questions and a mock test to assess your own ability. By taking these tests and checking your answers, you will be able to identify your strengths and weaknesses. This means that you can adjust your preparation to focus on your weaknesses and turn them into your strengths.

While learning the techniques needed to answer the questions is vital, it's also important to pay attention to the *types* of questions that appear in both tests and familiarise yourself with them.

Ask yourself the following for each kind of question:

- How is it structured?
- What exactly is it asking?

From here, you can highlight exactly what you need to know for each kind of question. Then, you can look at each area of the tests and tick them off as you go, knowing that you've covered them adequately. By doing this, you can be sure that you've covered everything that you need to know for the QTS skills tests.

What will I find in this book?

This book will cover three main areas related to becoming a teacher and acquiring QTS. The first and second parts of this book will cover the QTS literacy and QTS numeracy skills tests. This will include detailed analysis of all the kinds of problems and questions you might face, as well as some sample questions to help you identify and strengthen your weaknesses. Finally, a mock test will be offered as a final chance to test all of your skills. Answers to all the questions will be available at the end of each section.

The final part of this book will focus on the other aspects of becoming a teacher. In particular, it will cover the other required skills and traits for becoming a teacher, how to apply for teacher training, as well as what to expect from the experience. This means that, once you've passed the QTS skills tests, you have an idea of what you will face and how to take your training to the next stage.

With the help of this book, as well as determination and preparation on your part, you should have no problem passing the QTS skills tests. Our guidance will put you one step closer to your dream role as a teacher!

Tips for passing the QTS skills tests

Practice!

The greatest accomplishments do not come easily. If they did, they wouldn't be great accomplishments at all. Hard work is absolutely necessary for achieving your dream role, so be ready to put the hours in and practice. However, don't just practice hard – make sure to practice smart as well. Focus on improving your weaknesses and learn exactly what the tests will ask of you. Devoting time to preparation is very important, but make sure to use your preparation time wisely.

Stay calm.

Losing focus and becoming overwhelmed by your preparation (or the test itself) can have a negative impact on your overall performance. Take your time with this book and work at your own pace. Do not book the tests until you feel fully prepared, since this may put unnecessary pressure on you. If stress still gets the better of you, consider learning some breathing techniques to calm your nerves. This will prove useful during your preparation and when it comes to sitting the tests.

Remember that by reading this book, and making use of its resources, you are already in a strong position. Be confident in your ability and you'll be able to keep calm from the beginning to the end of your tests.

Manage your time.

Time management is key to both preparation and the tests themselves. Figure out how much time you can devote to preparation each day, and consider drawing out a revision timetable to help you stay focused. Remember to include breaks and leisure time in this timetable; you need time away from your studies to prevent stress.

As for the tests, figure out how much time you have to complete each section. Use the mock tests to time yourself, and then work on sections that you aren't as confident in, to make sure you can complete those sections adequately and in good time. In the tests, try and answer the questions you find easiest first, so that you don't get caught up on the ones you struggle with.

THE QTS LITERACY SKILLS TEST

INTRODUCTION

What is the QTS literacy skills test?

The QTS literacy skills test is one of two tests which you must pass before becoming a teacher in England and Wales.

The literacy skills test is carried out on a computer. This means that you will have to type out your answers rather than write them on paper. The test takes about 45 minutes to complete, and can be taken at Learndirect centres which are found all over the country. Your first attempt is free of charge, but all subsequent attempts must be paid for. For this reason, it's certainly worthwhile to prepare well in advance of the test, and ensure you pass first time!

What am I being tested on?

The literacy skills test will assess your understanding of four main areas: spelling, punctuation, grammar and comprehension. There will be one section for each aspect, bringing the test to a total of four sections. However, the marks are not distributed evenly across all sections. Regardless, you should spend time learning all four sections, rather than specialising in just one or two and neglecting the others. This way you'll still be able to secure marks, regardless of what is asked of you.

What is the pass mark?

You need to score at least 60 per cent (%) in the literacy skills test in order to pass. The marks for each section are as follows:

Spelling	10 marks
Punctuation	15 marks
Grammar	10-12 marks (depending on the test)
Comprehension	10-12 marks (depending on the test)

For the grammar and comprehension sections, the marks may be distributed differently. If a test has 12 marks available for grammar, then the comprehension section should have 10 marks available, and vice versa.

Why is the test important?

In order to be a good teacher, you must possess adequate literacy skills. It's important to be able to set a good example for your students. It's also imperative that you can clearly and effectively communicate with your students, in good English. For example, a class may be reading an online article about the First World War. If a sentence is structured poorly, confuses meanings of words or contains misspellings, students may struggle to read and understand it. In this scenario, you may have to correct the material to make it easier for them to understand.

Similarly, strong comprehension skills will allow you to identify the key points of a passage or piece of text. In turn, you could explain these points to students who are struggling with the passage. These skills apply across all school subjects, so it's vital that all teachers have them at their disposal.

How can I prepare for the test?

Firstly, make use of the resources in this book. Each section will provide you with explanations for different devices and challenges that you might face in the literacy test, as well as practice questions and a mock test to assess your own ability. By taking these tests and checking your answers, you will be able to identify your strengths and weaknesses. This means that you can adjust your preparation to focus on your weaknesses and turn them into your strengths.

Secondly, remember that the test is taken on a computer rather than on paper. While you won't have to worry about handwriting, you will need to practice your typing skills, particularly for the spelling section of the test. Being able to type quickly is important, but what's vital is that you avoid mistyping. "Typos" will result in a loss of marks for the spelling section. If you find yourself struggling with typing, be sure to check each of your answers before moving on so that you correct any mistakes.

How should I use this book?

These chapters will discuss the four sections of the literacy skills test in great depth. Each chapter will begin with an explanation of what to expect from the section of the test, followed by a guide to performing effectively in each part. Where applicable, you will also learn the definitions of certain devices such as punctuation marks. Finally, each chapter will provide you with some sample questions to familiarise yourself with the structure of the test, as well as give you some practice in answering them.

Once you have read all of the material, made use of the practice questions and feel confident in your ability, it's time to attempt the mock test.

THE QTS
LITERACY
SKILLS TEST
SPELLING

Introduction

The spelling section of the literacy skills test will be the first that you face. You must complete this section first, and once completed you cannot return to it. There are 10 marks available for the spelling section, making it a considerable chunk of the overall test. Therefore, it's important to take the time to improve your spelling skills in preparation for it.

Good spelling isn't quite as important for teaching as other aspects of literacy such as grammar, punctuation and comprehension. Most modern word-processing software includes sophisticated spell-checking facilities, and so being able to spell well isn't as important for writing in general.

However, good spelling is still an important skill to have as a teacher. This is because you may need to correct a student's work to ensure that they don't develop poor spelling habits. Likewise, you need to be able to set a good example, so that students do not get confused about the work given to them.

For instance, if you provided students with material you've written for them to learn from, and it's riddled with spelling errors, it might be difficult for them to read. In the worst-case scenario, students might follow your lead and adopt your incorrect spelling as their own, which would have a negative impact on their learning. Therefore, a teacher should be able to identify incorrect spelling.

In addition, being able to help students with words that they cannot spell is important across specialisms. For these reasons, spelling skills are taken seriously and therefore they are assessed in the literacy skills test.

In this chapter, you will be given the materials needed to improve your spelling skills for the literacy skills test.

How is this section presented?

In the test, you will be given ten sentences, each with a word deleted from them. In their place will be an audio icon. You will be supplied with headphones so that you can listen to the word and then type it into the computer. You can listen to the word as many times as you like – you just need to click on the icon again to repeat it.

If you suffer from a hearing impairment, you can take a version of the test which doesn't involve listening to words being read out. In this version of the test, you will be given ten sentences – each with a word missing. Rather than listening to the deleted word, you will be provided with a number of choices. A question in this version of the test might appear as follows:

The head teacher demanded that the students were _ _ _ _ _ _ _ _ dressed for school.

- *appropriately*
- *approprietly*
- *appropriatly*
- *appropreetly*

In the sample questions section of this chapter, you will be provided materials to answer audio versions of the questions, as well as hearing impaired versions. A URL link to a web page for the sound files will be given.

Before attempting the sample questions, take a look at the following sections. These focus on some of the most difficult words that you may come across in the test, as well as some techniques for remembering the spelling.

Finally, make sure that you use British English spelling conventions for the test. The use of the American English –ize suffix is accepted, but other than that, you should be using British English spellings (e.g. "colour" instead of "color").

Difficult Words and Conventions

In the test, you will be expected to spell words that you'd likely face in the world of teaching. You probably won't need to be able to spell "deontology" or "larynx" very often, and so you won't be required to spell words of that kind. However, there are still difficult words that you may face in the literacy skills test. In this section, we will cover the tougher kinds of spelling.

Advice	Definite
Pronunciation	Profession
Sufficient	Mischievous
Ridiculed	Criticised
Sincere	Disastrous
Exaggerating	Environment
Queue	Separate
Argument	Received

Before continuing, take a look at the words above and try to spell them. Some of them are words which contain a double consonant, whilst others contain prefixes and suffixes. In this book, we will cover both of these spelling conventions. They can be rather tricky, and will likely appear in the test.

Prefixes and Suffixes

These are collections of letters which are assigned to the beginning or end of certain words. A prefix comes *before* the word, while a suffix comes at the *end* of it. Prefixes and suffixes are added onto pre-existing words to change their tense or usage.

A prefix is added to the beginning of a root word in order to create a new word (PRE = before).

Prefixes generally act in a straight-forward manner. Words with an added prefix will always remain unchanged in spelling. For example, when "appropriate" becomes "inappropriate," the prefix 'in-' is added, but the spelling remains unchanged.

PREFIX	EXAMPLES
Pre -	*Pre*view, *pre*caution, *pre*face
Re -	*Re*try, *re*absorb, *re*do, *re*align
Auto -	*Auto*biography, *auto*graph
Un -	*Un*happy, *un*able, *un*deniable
De -	*De*brief, *de*activate, *de*code
Sub -	*Sub*culture, *sub*marine
Trans -	*Trans*port, *trans*cribe, *trans*form
In -	*In*active, *in*ability, *in*voice
Dis -	*Dis*mantle, *dis*arm, *dis*agree
Im -	*Im*possible, *im*polite, *im*patient
Ir -	*Ir*regular, *Ir*responsible, *ir*rational
Il -	*Il*logical, *il*legal, *il*literate

Prefixes often make the root word have an opposite meaning. For example, adding the prefix 'in-' to 'active' makes it take the opposite meaning. 'Active' becomes 'inactive'.

A suffix is added to the end of a root word in order to create a new word.

In many cases, words don't undergo major changes when adding a suffix, but other words have to be spelt slightly differently. For example, when 'appropriate' becomes 'appropriately', the only change is the addition of the suffix '-ly'. However, when 'exaggerate' becomes 'exaggerating', the suffix '-ing' is added, but the 'e' at the end of the word is removed.

SUFFIX	EXAMPLES
- Less	*Hopeless, powerless, senseless*
- Ment	*Department, payment, commitment*
- Er	*Attacker, keeper, bouncer*
- Ness	*Effectiveness, firmness, illness*
- Ity	*Abnormality, credibility, objectivity*
- Ly	*Abruptly, amazingly, barely*
- Able	*Accountable, unavoidable, breakable*
- Ful	*Bashful, delightful, forgetful*
- Ing	*Allowing, timing, jumping, building*
- Ed	*Abandoned, adapted, encouraged*
- Ise	*Criticise, familiarise, globalise*
- Ible	*Accessible, destructible, reversible*

Read the following words and try adding appropriate prefixes and/or suffixes to each. Some words will have multiple prefixes and suffixes that can be applied.

Separate	Definite	Real
Professional	Commit	Harass
Necessary	Sufficient	Important
Consider	Except	Exempt
Content	Permit	Facilitate
Applicable	Disappoint	Approximate
Own	Questionable	Enthusiastic
Assure	Secure	Practical

Generally speaking, when a word ends with an 'e' and can be suffixed with '-ing', the 'e' is removed when the suffix is added. 'Separate' becomes 'separating', 'facilitate' becomes 'facilitating' and 'equate' becomes 'equating'.

When adding '-ly' to a word that ends with an 'e', the 'e' usually remains in place. For example, 'approximate' becomes 'approximately'.

However, if the word usually ends with '-le', then adding the suffix '-ly' removes the 'e'. So, 'applicable' becomes 'applicably'.

Also bear in mind that many words can have a prefix as well as a suffix, such as 'unquestionably' or 'unimportantly'.

Double Consonants

Words which contain double consonants are among the most difficult to learn and are often incorrectly spelt by plenty of people. This is mainly because there are no clear patterns that you can discern from them. Essentially, you will need to learn each double consonant word individually, because there are no simple rules to follow.

Unfortunately, you will probably come across double consonants in the spelling section of the test, since they are quite common in everyday language. Keep a list of words that contain double consonants and practise spelling them. Use this list to get started:

Alliteration	Irreplaceable	Approximate	Disappointing
Professional	Embarrass	Intermittent	Beginning
Gorilla	Tomorrow	Appreciate	Belligerent
Anniversary	Intelligent	Pressure	Communicate
Annunciation	Accelerate	Commodity	Accomplish
Access	Consciousness	Annoying	Brilliant
Application	Dilemma	Etiquette	Collect
Appraisal	Rebellious	Immaculate	Intellectual

As you can see, there aren't any clear patterns which form to make memorable rules. In particular, be careful for words which use multiple sets of double consonants, such as 'accommodate' and 'embarrass.' In these cases, two sets of consonants are double, but other words do not follow this rule. Both "gorilla" and "dilemma" have a single pair of consonants which follows from a single consonant.

While most spellings are strictly correct or incorrect, there are some exceptions. In the spelling test, both 'biased' and 'biassed' are acceptable, as are both 'focused' and 'focussed.' Whichever spelling you choose, try to be consistent.

Homophones

These are words which sound the same, but are spelt differently and have different meanings. If you are going to be sitting the audio version of the spelling test, homophones can be particularly tricky, since hearing the word won't necessarily point out the correct spelling. In order to answer questions which involve homophonic words, you will have to know what each of the variations mean and then examine the sentence the word has been taken from. From there, you can figure out which spelling is appropriate.

The four sets of homophones which you need to pay the most attention to are:

There/Their/They're	To/Two/Too	Your/You're	Whose/Who's

These words are notorious for being confusing, even amongst adults. It's also possible that you will need to answer a question on them in the test.

THERE

- Used to denote location, place or position.
- *"The train station can be found **there**."*
- *"**There** is a cat nearby."*

THEIR

- Used to denote ownership (usually a group of things' ownership).
- *"**Their** shoes were muddy from cutting through the nearby field."*
- *"It was **their** responsibility to lock **their** computers while they were away."*

THEY'RE

- A contraction of *'they are'.*

- 'They' is a group of things, whilst 'are' is used to denote what is currently the case for the group.

- *"**They are** going to the shops." = "**They're** going to the shops."*

- *"The students don't feel confident about the test, but **they're** going to do just fine."*

TO

- Used to denote motion or a change in condition.

- *"I went **to** the shops."*

- *"Things went from bad **to** worse."*

TWO

- The number '2'

- *"There were **two** dogs hanging around outside."*

TOO

- Used to denote excess. Can replace the word *"also"* or *"as well."*

- *"There were **too** many people on the train."*

- *"It was later decided that James could come **too**."*

YOUR

- Used to denote ownership.

- *"This is **your** room."*

- *"**Your** payment is overdue."*

YOU'RE

- A contraction of 'you are'.

- *"**You're** going to the shops." = "**You are** going to the shops."*

WHOSE

- Used to denote ownership.

- *"**Whose** shoes are these?"*

WHO'S

- A contraction of 'who is'.

- *"**Who's** going to clean up this mess?"*

These are just a few examples showing how these homophonic words are different from one another. When you come across these during reading, try and take apart the sentence that the word is in, and figure out why it is spelt in that way. In the test, you should do the same. Read the entire sentence to understand what the word is being used to do, and then choose the correct spelling.

Be aware that there are other homophones too, such as:

Practice/Practise	Wear/Where
Air/Heir	Aisle/I'll/Isle
Board/Bored	Fir/Fur
Ate/Eight	Fair/Fare

The best way to learn these is by familiarising yourself with their meanings and usage in a sentence. This way, you will be able to tell which spelling is suitable given the sentence surrounding it.

Longer Words

On the surface, longer words appear to be the toughest part of spelling. After all, a longer word has more letters in it, and therefore there is more chance of spelling it incorrectly. However, longer words can actually be quite easy to spell once you learn how to handle them.

The best way to approach a longer word is by dissecting it into smaller chunks. This can be done by dividing a word into <u>syllables</u>:

Appropriately = Ap-pro-pri-ate-ly

By doing this, you can remember smaller groups of letters rather than one large block. This can be particularly useful for remembering some words which contain double consonants. Try using this method on your list of difficult words, or try it with the following:

Invariable	Extricable	Antagonise
Ferocious	Conjecture	Dissonance
Excruciating	Pernicious	Reparation

'I' before 'E'

This might be the most infamous convention in the English language, due to its apparent concreteness, despite having plenty of exceptions.

Generally, the rule is considered to be "i before e, except after c." However, there are a number of exceptions to this rule, such as:

Eight   Height   Forfeit

This means that the rule has to be adjusted slightly to "i before e, except after c, if the sound is ee." This means that if the word has an 'ee' sound (like how it sounds in the word "seek") as well as a c before it, then the 'ei' spelling must be used.

For example, the word 'perceive' has an 'ee' sound. It also has a 'c' before the 'ee' sound. Therefore, the spelling must be 'ei' rather than 'ie'.

With this amended rule, words such as 'eight' and 'forfeit' can be remembered with their correct spelling in mind, while 'perceive' and 'receive' have an 'ei' spelling due to the 'c'.

Spelling Tips

One of the best ways to improve your spelling skills is to keep a list of words that you find difficult to spell, and then attempt to spell them every so often. If possible, record yourself saying the words, so that you can listen to them via speakers or headphones.

After recording these words, play them back to yourself repeatedly and try writing them down or typing them on a computer. Once you're confident that you've mastered the spelling of a word, cross it off of your list and move onto other words.

Another way to supplement your spelling ability is to read regularly. By reading fiction and non-fiction, you will come into contact with more words. When you encounter a new word, try to spell it without looking at it. If you struggle with the spelling, add it to your list of difficult words.

As time goes on, you will start to notice patterns in spelling which might make it easier to remember rules, such as the ones which apply to prefixes and suffixes. If possible, try to read materials which are suitable for teachers, including government documents. By reading these, you will become more familiar with the language used in teaching. Since the questions in the spelling section will primarily feature words associated with teaching, reading these materials which put you in a much better position for answering questions in the spelling section.

Having a dictionary handy while practising will be extremely useful for learning homophones, since you will only be able to differentiate them by their meaning and usage in a sentence. Be sure to read the examples that the dictionary gives for each word.

If you are having difficulties with a word, try speaking it aloud and break it down into its syllables. You won't be able to do this in the actual test due to silent exam conditions, but you can do it during practice. However, remember that words aren't always spelled in the same way that they sound, but there are plenty of spellings which can be solved using this method.

There are also some tricks which will be useful across all kinds of conventions. A mnemonic can make some particularly unusual spellings easier to remember. For example:

*Rhythm – **R**eading **H**elps **Y**ou **T**hink **H**ard **M**ore*

Additionally, you can make analogies between certain words. For example, 'perceive', 'conceive' and 'receive' all sound similar, and they all share 'ceive' as part of their spelling. Look for more patterns like this during your reading.

Once you've read through this section and feel confident with some of the difficult words you might face, turn to the sample questions on the following pages.

Spelling – Sample Questions – Non-Audio Version

Use these sample questions to familiarise yourself with the spelling section of the test. Have a look at the questions before attempting them. Bear in mind that during the real test you will only have to answer ten spelling questions. More have been offered here as a means of practice.

1. There was no point in trying to _ _ _ _ _ _ _ _ _ _ _ _ _ _ _ _ with some of the younger pupils.

    - Reason
    - Reeson
    - Reasin
    - Reson

2. The changes to the school uniform _ _ _ _ _ _ _ _ _ _ _ _ _ _ a significant change in the school's attitude.

    - Repesented
    - Represented
    - Repreesented
    - Reppresented

3. Fortnightly _ _ _ _ _ _ _ _ _ _ _ _ _ _ _ with some of the worst-performing pupils were established.

    - Apraisals
    - Appraissals
    - Aprassals
    - Appraisals

4. An _ _ _ _ _ _ _ _ _ _ _ _ _ _ _ _ was expected at the end of the month.

- Insspection
- Innspection
- Inspection
- Inspecsion

5. The class seemed completely _ _ _ _ _ _ _ _ _ _ _ _ _ _ _ _ _.

- Uncontrollable
- Unncontrolable
- Uncontrolable
- Unconntrolable

6. One student had been held in detention for _ _ _ _ _ _ _ _ _ _ _ _ _ _ _ one of her classmates.

- Harasing
- Harrassing
- Harassing
- Harrasing

7. There was a _ _ _ _ _ _ _ _ _ _ _ _ _ _ effort made by the leadership team to improve standards.

- Conscious
- Conseeus
- Conshus
- Conscius

8. The school trip had been _ _ _ _ _ _ _ _ _ _ _ _ _ _ _.

    - Posponed
    - Postponed
    - Postpowned
    - Pusponed

9. It hadn't _ _ _ _ _ _ _ _ _ _ _ _ _ _ _ to them that they hadn't brought their keys.

    - Ocurred
    - Occured
    - Ocured
    - Occurred

10. There was a noticeable _ _ _ _ _ _ _ _ _ _ _ _ _ _ between the higher sets of students and the lower ones.

    - Distinction
    - Distincsion
    - Distintion
    - Destinction

11. The school's leadership team had come to a _ _ _ _ _ _ _ _ _ _ _ _ _ _ _.

    - Dision
    - Decision
    - Decission
    - Dicision

12. Students had _ _ _ _ _ _ _ _ _ _ _ _ _ _ _ _ progress.

- Demonnstrated
- Demmonstrated
- Demonstrated
- Demonsstrated

13. _ _ _ _ _ _ _ _ _ _ _ _ _ _ _ _ would no longer be tolerated.

- Absence
- Abscence
- Absense
- Absince

14. The support for the new initiative was _ _ _ _ _ _ _ _ _ _ _ _ _ _ _ _ _.

- Overwelming
- Overwhelming
- Overwellming
- Overwhellming

15. The classroom was far _ _ _ _ _ _ _ _ _ _ _ _ _ _ _ _ loud for any work to be done.

- To
- Too
- Two
- Toe

16. The music class began to learn some new _ _ _ _ _ _ _ _ _ _ _ _ _ _ _ _ _ patterns.

- Rithmic
- Rhythimic
- Rithmyc
- Rhythmic

17. A _ _ _ _ _ _ _ _ _ _ _ _ _ _ _ _ _ amount of time was spent planning for each lesson.

- Considerible
- Considarable
- Consederable
- Considerable

18. Students found learning about the Romans to be _ _ _ _ _ _ _ _ _ _ _ _ _ _ _ _ _ _.

- Exiting
- Exciting
- Exsiting
- Exciteng

19. The lack of revision materials made pupils _ _ _ _ _ _ _ _ _ _ _ _ _ _ _ _ to failure.

- Suseptible
- Susiptible
- Susceptible
- Suseptable

20. The behaviour of students while on the trip had to be

---------------------.

- Excemplary
- Exemplory
- Exemplory
- Exemplary

21. The problem had to be _____ as soon as possible.

- Adresed
- Addressed
- Addresed
- Adressed

22. There was no point in continuing the lesson until the arguing between students had been _____.

- Resolved
- Rezolved
- Risolved
- Ressolved

23. Poor discipline caused the fire drill to be _____.

- Chaotic
- Kayotic
- Caotic
- Keyotic

24. Any decline in standards would be _ _ _ _ _ _ _ _ _ _ _ _ _ _ _ _ _ _ .

- Unnacceptable
- Unaceptable
- Unacceptable
- Unexceptable

25. Rewards were offered to _ _ _ _ _ _ _ _ _ _ _ _ _ _ _ _ _ students to work harder.

- Incourage
- Encourage
- Encurrage
- Encurage

26. _ _ _ _ _ _ _ _ _ _ _ _ _ _ _ _ grades had improved on the previous year.

- They're
- There
- Their
- Thier

27. The inspection had been a _ _ _ _ _ _ _ _ _ _ _ _ _ _ _ _ _ _ .

- Sucess
- Suces
- Succes
- Success

28. It was ------------------ how hard the maths department had worked to improve grades.

- Unbelievable
- Unbeleevable
- Unbeleivable
- Unbilivable

29. Sports day was ------------------- due to heavy rain.

- Canceled
- Cansilled
- Cancceled
- Cancelled

30. Summer activities were organised to take place during the ------------------.

- Holliday
- Holeday
- Huliday
- Holiday

Spelling – Sample Questions – Audio Version

For this version of the audio test, you will need access to the internet as well as a pair of headphones or some kind of speakers. Sound files for this section can be found at http://www.qtsspellingtest.co.uk/.

1. There was no point in trying to _ _ _ _ _ _ _ _ _ _ _ _ _ _ _ _ with some of the younger pupils.

2. The changes to the school uniform _ _ _ _ _ _ _ _ _ _ _ _ _ _ _ _ a significant change in the school's attitude.

3. Fortnightly _ _ _ _ _ _ _ _ _ _ _ _ _ _ _ with some of the worst-performing pupils were established.

4. An _ _ _ _ _ _ _ _ _ _ _ _ _ _ _ _ was expected at the end of the month.

5. The class seemed completely _ _ _ _ _ _ _ _ _ _ _ _ _ _ _ _.

6. One student had been held in detention for _ _ _ _ _ _ _ _ _ _ _ _ _ _ _ one of her classmates.

7. There was a _ _ _ _ _ _ _ _ _ _ _ _ _ _ _ _ effort made by the leadership team to improve standards.

8. The school trip had been _ _ _ _ _ _ _ _ _ _ _ _ _ _ _ _.

9. It hadn't _ _ _ _ _ _ _ _ _ _ _ _ _ _ _ _ to them that they hadn't brought their keys.

10. There was a noticeable _ _ _ _ _ _ _ _ _ _ _ _ _ _ _ between the higher sets of students and the lower ones.

11. The school's leadership team had come to a _ _ _ _ _ _ _ _ _ _ _ _ _ _ _ _.

12. Students had _ _ _ _ _ _ _ _ _ _ _ _ _ _ _ _ _ progress.

13. _ _ _ _ _ _ _ _ _ _ _ _ _ _ _ _ _ would no longer be tolerated.

14. The support for the new initiative was _ _ _ _ _ _ _ _ _ _ _ _ _ _ _ _ _ _.

15. The classroom was far _ _ _ _ _ _ _ _ _ _ _ _ _ _ _ _ loud for any work to be done.

16. The music class began to learn some new _ _ _ _ _ _ _ _ _ _ _ _ _ _ _ _ patterns.

17. A _ _ _ _ _ _ _ _ _ _ _ _ _ _ _ _ amount of time was spent planning for each lesson.

18. Students found learning about the Romans to be _ _ _ _ _ _ _ _ _ _ _ _ _ _ _ _ _.

19. The lack of revision materials made pupils _ _ _ _ _ _ _ _ _ _ _ _ _ _ _ _ to failure.

20. The behaviour of students while on the trip had to be
_ _ _ _ _ _ _ _ _ _ _ _ _ _ _ _ _.

21. The problem had to be _ _ _ _ _ _ _ _ _ _ _ _ _ _ _ _ as soon as possible.

22. There was no point in continuing the lesson until the arguing between students had been _ _ _ _ _ _ _ _ _ _ _ _ _ _ _ _.

23. Poor discipline caused the fire drill to be _ _ _ _ _ _ _ _ _ _ _ _ _ _ _ _.

24. Any decline in standards would be _ _ _ _ _ _ _ _ _ _ _ _ _ _ _ _.

25. Rewards were offered to _ _ _ _ _ _ _ _ _ _ _ _ _ _ _ _ students to work harder.

26. _ _ _ _ _ _ _ _ _ _ _ _ _ _ _ _ grades had improved on the previous year.

27. The inspection had been a _ _ _ _ _ _ _ _ _ _ _ _ _ _ _ _ _.

28. It was _ _ _ _ _ _ _ _ _ _ _ _ _ _ _ _ how hard the maths department had worked to improve grades.

29. Sports day was _ _ _ _ _ _ _ _ _ _ _ _ _ _ _ _ due to heavy rain.

30. Summer activities were organised to take place during the _ _ _ _ _ _ _ _ _ _ _ _ _ _ _ _ _ _.

Spelling – Answers

1. There was no point in trying to **reason** with some of the younger pupils.

2. The changes to the school uniform **represented** a significant change in the school's attitude.

3. Fortnightly **appraisals** with some of the worst-performing pupils were established.

4. An **inspection** was expected at the end of the month.

5. The class seemed completely **uncontrollable**.

6. One student had been held in detention for **harassing** one of her classmates.

7. There was a **conscious** effort made by the leadership team to improve standards.

8. The school trip had been **postponed**.

9. It hadn't **occurred** to them that they hadn't brought their keys.

10. There was a noticeable **distinction** between the higher sets of students and the lower ones.

11. The school's leadership team had come to a **decision**.

12. Students had **demonstrated** progress.

13. **Absence** would no longer be tolerated.

14. The support for the new initiative was **overwhelming**.

15. The classroom was far **too** loud for any work to be done.

16. The music class began to learn some new **rhythmic** patterns.

17. A **considerable** amount of time was spent planning for each lesson.

18. Students found learning about the Romans to be **exciting**.

19. The lack of revision materials made pupils **susceptible** to failure.

20. The behaviour of students while on the trip had to be **exemplary**.

21. The problem had to be **addressed** as soon as possible.

22. There was no point in continuing the lesson until the arguing between students had been **resolved**.

23. Poor discipline caused the fire drill to be **chaotic**.

24. Any decline in standards would be **unacceptable**.

25. Rewards were offered to **encourage** students to work harder.

26. **Their** grades had improved on the previous year.

27. The inspection had been a **success**.

28. It was **unbelievable** how hard the maths department had worked to improve grades.

29. Sports day was **cancelled** due to heavy rain.

30. Summer activities were organised to take place during the **holiday**.

Conclusion

The spelling section of the literacy skills test can be rather difficult, since you have to learn spellings for a lot of words by heart. Thankfully, the test won't throw any particularly nasty spellings at you – just words that you're likely to come across as a teacher.

So long as you've followed the advice in this section and attempted some sample questions, you can be confident in your ability.

When you feel ready, move onto the next chapter, which focuses on punctuation.

THE QTS
LITERACY
SKILLS TEST
PUNCTUATION

Introduction

Punctuation is an extremely important part of literacy. Without it, sentences don't form properly and the point of a text can be lost in a block of words. In addition, punctuation signifies the flow of a sentence or paragraph; it allows you to get a feel for a passage, and can accentuate key points. For this reason, punctuation is a significant aspect of the literacy skills test.

A firm grasp on punctuation is important for reading and writing, and therefore a teacher needs to be aware of the various devices at play. A teacher with a thorough understanding of punctuation will be able to help students to understand a text if they are struggling with it, and will be able to spot poorly-written materials when preparing lessons.

Punctuation skills are also useful when reading for yourself. For example, knowing that a colon is used to begin a list may help you to better understand the structure of the paragraph. Likewise, an understanding of how parentheses (brackets) work, will help you to separate the key points of a text from the minor side-points.

In this chapter, you will become comfortable with paragraphing, colons, semi-colons and other punctuation tools.

What should I expect from this section?

The punctuation section of the literacy skills test is worth 15 marks. This is more than any other section, and therefore you must devote a considerable amount of time to it. While it is advised to give each section an equal amount of attention during preparation and the test, make sure you cover punctuation thoroughly. If you struggle with punctuation, you should make it your priority to learn the punctuation marks and what their uses are.

In the test, you will be presented with a single text with its punctuation deleted. To gain marks, you will need to correctly place punctuation in the passage.

There will be a total of 15 punctuation omissions in the text, one for each available mark. The test allows for more than 15 punctuation corrections to be made even if they are unnecessary, but incorrect additions will be penalised. Essentially, over-punctuation is acceptable so long as it remains consistent.

Sentence Structure

Before continuing, it is worthwhile discussing the importance of punctuation in the context of sentence structure. Sentences are made of clauses – short passages of text which usually encompass one main point. These clauses, and therefore the overall sentences, are defined by punctuation. This means that without punctuation, proper sentences would never exist.

Clauses in a sentence can be separated by commas, and sentences themselves are defined by full stops, exclamation marks and question marks. Poor placement of punctuation (or no placement at all!) can lead to confusing sentences. In some cases, the entire meaning of a sentence can be changed by punctuation.

Ambiguity can stem from poor use of punctuation, and can mislead the reader. Therefore, it is vital that a teacher can structure sentences properly.

Punctuation Marks and Devices

This section will cover the punctuation marks and devices that you could face in the literacy skills test. Not all of them will show up, and it's entirely possible that common ones such as full stops and commas will appear more than once. However, it is important to read the explanations for each, in case any of them appear.

Full Stop (.)

Full stops are used to mark the end of a sentence. Since a sentence generally contains one main point (clause), you should add a full stop when the main point changes.

This is a sentence with two full stops deleted:

> *The students were allowed outside after the rain had stopped ten minutes later the ground had dried and the playing field was re-opened*

It should read as:

> *The students were allowed outside after the rain had stopped. Ten minutes later the ground had dried and the playing field was re-opened.*

Firstly, there should always be a full stop, question mark or exclamation mark at the end of a passage. This explains the addition of the second full stop at the end of the text.

Furthermore, a full stop has been added in the middle of the text. This is to separate two different points. Because these are main points, they deserve their own sentence.

A sentence is usually complete when it has at least one verb (e.g. stopped) and at least one subject (e.g. students, rain). These combined usually make up a clause, and therefore there will be at least one clause in a sentence.

Note: A sentence can have multiple clauses. These are known as subordinate clauses. However, a sentence can only have one main clause. If you can see more than one main clause, then you probably need to create a new sentence.

Comma (,)

A comma is often used to distinguish main clauses from secondary or subordinate clauses. Commas are frequently misused and therefore you shouldn't use them unless you are sure that they're appropriate. Instead, resort to employing full stops if you aren't sure whether a comma would be correct. If part of a text feels complete, or contains a subject and verb, it is safe to define it with a full stop.

<u>For example:</u>

> *He mustered a sigh of relief, his car was right where he left it in the car park.*

The comma here is used <u>incorrectly</u>. The first part of the sentence *(He mustered a sigh of relief)* contains a verb (mustered) and a subject (he). Therefore, it should be its own sentence:

> *He mustered a sigh of relief. His car was right where he left it in the car park.*

Commas can also be used to add a preface to a sentence, with a word such as 'however' and 'unfortunately.' This can be used to set the tone of a sentence and link it to a previous sentence:

> *His car was right where he left it in the car park. Unfortunately, two of the windows had been smashed.*

These sentence adverbs add context to the sentence which follows it. In this case, use a comma after the sentence adverb.

Here are some other sentence adverbs, which require a comma to be placed after them:

> Honestly, …   Clearly, …   Frankly, …
> Curiously, …   Sadly, …   Coincidentally, …
> Afterwards, …   Suddenly, …   In contrast, …

Commas are also used to separate the items of a list which appear in the text rather than as bullet points.

For example:

> *The damage to the car included two smashed windows, a slashed tyre, dents on the bonnet and a snapped aerial.*

Each item in the list is followed by a comma to distinguish them. Generally, the final item on the list uses the connective 'and' rather than another comma (e.g. *dents on the bonnet **and** a snapped aerial*).

Commas can be used to change the order of a sentence. By changing how the sentence is structured, variety can be added to the text.

For example, read the following sentence:

> *Orderly queues were formed outside of the main hall in order to prevent congestion in the corridors.*

This can be restructured using a comma to read as:

> *In order to prevent congestion in the corridors, orderly queues were formed outside of the main hall.*

Both sentences make sense and flow well, but variety can keep a sentence interesting.

Another use of the comma is to embed clauses into a main clause. This is done to add extra information without making the sentence ambiguous.

For example:

> *The boys, wearing suits, couldn't climb over the fence.*

Without commas, this would read differently:

> *The boys wearing suits couldn't climb over the fence.*

There is a slight difference in meaning between these two statements. The subject of the first sentence is 'the boys'. In the second sentence, the subject is 'the boys wearing suits'.

The difference between the two sentences is subtle but important, since the use of commas in the first sentence creates an embedded clause. In this case, it works as an explanation: that the boys couldn't climb over the fence because they were wearing suits.

In the second sentence, all of the boys wearing suits could not climb over the fence, but this could be due to any reason. For instance, they could be too short to climb it. By adding the embedded clause, extra information is added to the sentence. This makes the sentence clearer overall.

In this case, the embedded clause is 'wearing suits'. This information could have been included in another way, such as with parentheses (brackets) or by using dashes. However, both would interrupt the flow of the sentence:

> *The boys (wearing suits) couldn't climb over the fence.*
> *The boys – wearing suits – couldn't climb over the fence.*

Therefore, the embedded clause is the best choice for this sentence.

In order to spot this use of commas during the test, look for pieces of additional information placed into sentences which would function on their own.

For example:

> *The boys couldn't climb over the fence.*

This functions as a complete sentence, but if the added clause was embedded without commas, it may look messy or confusing. In these cases, it is best to add a comma.

In addition to whole clauses, sometimes individual words are embedded into a sentence. These operate in the same way:

> *The boys, **understandably**, couldn't climb over the fence.*
>
> ***Understandably**, the boys couldn't climb over the fence.*
>
> *The boys couldn't climb over the fence, **understandably**.*

Finally, commas are used when writing dialogue. The comma comes after the final word of text, before the quotation marks appear:

> *Mrs Brown exclaimed, "Students are failing to understand the importance of the First World War."*

In other cases, the dialogue may be separated by directions about the speaker and their tone. In this scenario the commas are placed differently.

> *"Students are failing to understand the importance of the First World War," Mrs Brown exclaimed. "This must change in the near future."*

If this structure is used, then the comma appears at the end of the first piece of dialogue, before the speech marks end and the speech directions are given.

Paragraphs

Paragraphs are used to break up larger pieces of text. Generally speaking, a new paragraph is needed when the text switches to a new idea or theme. There are no set rules on how long a paragraph should be: sometimes they will only be a couple of lines long, but on other occasions a longer paragraph may be necessary.

Good paragraphing skills form the bedrock for strong flow and sentence structure, since they allow you to separate your ideas. In many ways, a good paragraph will take the same form as a good story or essay, but on a smaller scale.

Firstly, a topic sentence is needed to set the stage for the content of the paragraph. These topic sentences serve as a summary, so that the reader knows where they stand in the paragraph.

After the topic sentence, the rest of the paragraph should be working to reinforce the initial statement of the topic sentence.

Finally, the end of the paragraph might include a conclusion sentence which briefly sums up its focus.

In the test, you may need to add paragraphs to a piece of text. To answer questions of this kind, pay attention to the larger chunks of text. If you see a change in tone, topic or time/place, then it may be necessary to start a new paragraph.

If you aren't sure whether a new paragraph is necessary in the test, take a look at how many other punctuation additions you've made. If you've already added 15 vital pieces of punctuation, then it probably isn't the case that you need the new paragraph.

Colon (:)

For the most part, colons only have one use: to introduce a list. This applies to an in-text list, such as:

> *There were three entrances to the hall: the double doors leading from the lobby, the side entrance from a main corridor and the fire door leading onto the staff car park.*

Colons are also used to introduce bulleted lists:

> *There were three entrances to the hall:*
> - *The double doors leading from the lobby;*
> - *The side entrance from the main corridor;*
> - *The fire door leading onto the staff car park.*

Colons can also be used to introduce a quotation:

> *However, the inspector thought differently: 'Students clearly don't know how to behave in lessons.'*

Finally, colons can be used to add an explanation to a statement:

> *There was no reason to believe that the students were incapable: they had all completed their homework and performed well in the tests, but were too shy to raise their hand to answer questions.*

Semi-Colon (;)

Unlike the other punctuation marks in this chapter, the semi-colon is very rarely necessary. Its role in language is to link two related sentences together. Generally speaking, it is used to make a text more varied or assist with the flow, but it isn't necessary. Many accomplished writers will never use semi-colons because it isn't part of their style, while others may use them frequently.

The first main use of a semi-colon is to join two related sentences together:

> *The understanding of the staff was that students were more than capable to complete the science test; in fact, many had already sat mock exams and performed well.*

These two parts of the sentence could have formed separate sentences:

> *The understanding of the staff was that students were more than capable of completing the science test. In fact, many had already sat mock exams and performed well.*

By joining them with a semi-colon, it's clear that they relate to one another.

The second use of a semi-colon is to mark the components of a list:

> *There were three entrances to the hall:*
> - *The double doors leading from the lobby;*
> - *The side entrance from the main corridor;*
> - *The fire door leading onto the staff car park.*

Excluding the final point, each item on the bulleted list is suffixed with a semi-colon.

Question Mark (?)

Question marks are used to signify that the sentence asks a question. Apart from this detail, it functions in the same way as a full stop, showing the end of a sentence:

> *Could there be another explanation as to why standards are falling?*

Sometimes a sentence will imply a question, but will not contain a question mark. This happens when the subject of the sentence comes before the verb:

> *I could ask if they would be able to stay behind for ten minutes to finish the mock test.*

Exclamation Mark (!)

An exclamation mark is used to show commands or other statements which are either forceful or surprising. It is mostly used in dialogue to express a raised voice, but it can also appear in ordinary text as well. Like the question mark, it operates in the same way as a full stop: it signifies the end of a sentence.

> *"Stop right there!" Jordan shouted.*

Parentheses (Brackets)

Brackets are used to denote an aside or other additional information without disrupting the flow of the sentence. Usually these details aren't absolutely vital, but are added for extra clarification. The contents inside the brackets are usually afterthoughts.

Brackets always occur in pairs. If they are opened, they need to be shut:

> *There were a number of us (perhaps fifteen or so) waiting at reception.*

Capital Letters (R, T, U, etc.)

A capital letter always appears at the start of a sentence:

> *Research has shown that students who are allowed to drink water in lessons perform better.*

Capital letters are also used for the names of people and places (proper nouns):

> *This was the only hotel in Paris which Henry could stay at.*

Dash (–)

A dash is used to separate information:

> *There were a number of people on the school tennis court – none of them were playing tennis.*

Be sure not to be confuse dashes with hyphens (a dash line is longer).

Hyphen (-)

A hyphen is used to combine two words into a form of compound word. A compound word with a hyphen is called a hyphenated compound:

Well-adjusted	So-called	Long-term
Old-fashioned	Absent-minded	Re-election
In-depth	Mother-in-law	Self-service

Hyphens are shorter than dashes, so make sure not to get the two of them confused. Since hyphens have more to do with spelling than punctuation, it's unlikely that you will have to add hyphens into a passage during the test. However, it pays to know what they are and how they work so that you have a better understanding of what a dash is.

Speech Marks (" ")

Speech marks are used to show that a voice other than the narrator's is speaking. This will usually be used for dialogue:

> *"We could begin this assembly early if it suits you," Mrs Brown suggested.*

Quotation Marks (' ')

Quotation marks can be used to show quotations in a text (similar to dialogue). Additionally, they can be used to add emphasis to certain words and phrases:

> *While there was no tangible risk for the work, workers were still offered 'hazard pay' just in case.*

Ellipsis (...)

An ellipsis is a set of three dots (full stops) which can add suspense, leave a sentence hanging or show interruptions or missing words.

> *Students showed complete disregard for the new Citizenship lessons... they were more willing to sit through Maths.*

Punctuation Tips

As previously mentioned, some elements of punctuation come down to personal taste. For example, some writers will never use semi-colons, while others will use them frequently. Neither of these approaches are right or wrong: some parts of punctuation are entirely subjective.

However, it is important to be consistent in your use of punctuation marks. By this we mean that you should build a style of writing in which a punctuation mark is used in the same way every time it appears. For example, the use of speech marks and quotation marks should be separated in your work, perhaps using speech marks purely for dialogue, and using quotation marks for quotes and emphasis. In theory, you could use either punctuation mark for any of those functions, since they are mostly interchangeable. The key is to be consistent in how you use them, so that you do not confuse the reader.

Let's say that a reader comes across speech marks in your work, and has already encountered them before in a piece of text you have written, proofread or edited. If your use of speech marks has been consistent, they can expect the text in speech marks to be like the other instances of speech marks that they have read in your work.

While aspects of punctuation depend on personal style, there are some uses of punctuation which may simply be correct or incorrect. In particular, the use of full stops, capital letters and colons/semi-colons are fairly standard, and therefore you should take the time to learn their rules and how they should be implemented.

In the test, remember that there are only 15 essential pieces of punctuation that you'll need to add to the text. Count the additions you have made as you go, to make sure that you've secured as many marks as possible. If you find that you've only added 12 pieces of punctuation to the text, then you need to find 3 more before you finish the section.

Punctuation 'Cheat Sheet'

Full stop (.)	A punctuation mark used to end a sentence after at least one clause is present. *The students were allowed outside after the rain had stopped.*
Comma (,)	A punctuation mark used to indicate a pause between parts of sentences or to separate items into a list format. *Once the rain had stopped, the students were allowed outside.*
Paragraphs	A way of breaking up text in order for the passage to flow better. Each paragraph usually deals with a different theme or idea. Indicated by a new or indented line. *The students were allowed outside after the rain had stopped.* *10 minutes later, the ground had dried and the playing field was re-opened.*

Colon (:)	A punctuation mark used to join sentences, introduce lists, introduce a quotation or introduce explanations.
	There were a number of things available that evening: tea, coffee, cakes and biscuits. (List)
	The parents, however, had taken issue with the new rules:
	"The decision to make uniform discipline stricter is absolutely draconian." (Introducing a quotation)
	The solution was actually rather simple: they just weren't looking in the right places for it.
	(Introducing an explanation)
Semi-colon (;)	A semi-colon is used to separate longer sentences but still reads as one complete sentence, or to link two closely related sentences.
	The team had won almost all of their matches in the tournament despite their injuries; their manager and coach were both incredibly impressed.
Question mark (?)	A question mark is used to indicate a question.
	Could the solution be to enforce stricter rules regarding uniform?
Exclamation mark (!)	An exclamation mark is used to show a command or something that is forceful or surprising.
	The project was exceptional!

Parentheses (brackets)	A punctuation mark used to signify an explanation or afterthought without breaking the flow of the sentence. *The car (if you could call it that) could barely start, and it took five minutes to finally leave the car park.*
Capital Letter (R, T, O)	Used for the first letter at the start of a sentence, and also for proper nouns (the names of people, places etc). *<u>T</u>here was only one hotel in <u>P</u>aris that <u>H</u>enry was prepared to stay at.*
Dash (–)	A dash is used to separate information. It is stronger than a comma, but not as formal as a colon. Not to be confused with a hyphen (a dash line is longer). *There were a number of instruments strewn across the music room <u>–</u> too many to tidy in an hour.*
Hyphen (-)	A hyphen is used to join words. This usually means they have a combined meaning. *Over<u>-</u>punctuation in the test is generally accepted.*
Speech mark (" ")	Speech marks are generally used to denote dialogue in the text, or a voice which does not belong to the writer/narrator. *<u>"</u>I'm pleased with the grades that I got,<u>"</u> Nazeem exclaimed, <u>"</u>but I still wish I had worked harder.<u>"</u>*

Quotation mark (' ')	A punctuation mark used to add emphasis to a certain phrase. It can also be used to highlight a piece of text which comes from another source a.k.a. a quotation.
	The 'competition' was hardly that at all, since one team dominated every match.
	(Adding emphasis)
	However, the implications of the report were worrying, since 'students showed complete disregard for the new Citizenship lessons.'
	(Quoting a source)
Ellipsis (...)	An ellipsis is a set of three dots (full stops) which can add suspense, leave a sentence hanging, show interruptions or missing words. This can also be used to shorten quotations.
	'Students showed complete disregard for the new Citizenship lessons... they were more willing to sit through Maths.'

Punctuation – Sample Questions

In the test, you will be given a single passage with most of its punctuation missing. You will need to add fifteen separate pieces of punctuation to the passage: one for each mark available. Use the following three sample questions to familiarise yourself with what might appear in the real test.

In the actual test, you will have to insert punctuation using the computer. For this book, you will have to write the punctuation in, using a pen or pencil. If you find a word which requires a capital letter, circle or underline it and write "capital" or "cap" in the margin. If a new paragraph is needed, put two forward slashes (//) before the first word of the new paragraph.

1.

So far seventeen students have been placed under observation, with at least five of them at risk of temporary suspension in particular, jordans suspension was being discussed by the leadership team his bad behaviour was considered among the worst. However the greater issue at play was that none of the teachers in the Science department could control the students. the headteacher has been reminded that teaching isn't purely about knowledge and the ability to put new ideas across it's equally important to be able to earn the respect of the class, and respect them in return A strong, mutual agreement between a teacher and their students is vital for success in lessons.

Mrs Brown reassured staff and parents that further training would take place to make sure teachers were able to handle the more excitable and troublesome classes Making sure that the school is a safe and efficient environment for students and teachers is still a high priority

2.

There were many complaints from students in the aftermath of changes to the school uniform The changes to the uniform would be coming into effect in the next school year, but new uniform is to be rolled out to students who need it at the moment any students who were representing the school at events there weren't many external events at that point in the year would be required to wear the new uniform. The colour of the school tie had been changed from a deep blue to bright purple, with an emblem at the top moreover, the jumpers worn were made brighter, resulting in a clash of colours. Another less controversial change was to rules regarding shoes. up until this point, the school had allowed dark brown shoes to be worn as well as black shoes the intention being that it allowed for more freedom in choosing what to wear. However, the school had taken a hardline stance against brown shoes only allowing black school shoes to be worn This would come into effect immediately

3.

According to the report given by witnesses on the schools playing field the incident had taken place as follows 1. henry had climbed the tree in the northwest corner of the field; 2. lalita and nazeem spotted Henry and told him he should climb down before he got hurt; 3. Henry shouted that Lalita and Nazeem were crybabies and needed to grow up; 4. Angered Lalita and Nazeem threw twigs and stones at Henry until he lost his grip on the tree branch; 5. Henry fell from the tree and sprained his ankle

Punctuation – Answers

1.

So far, seventeen students have been placed under observation, with at least five of them at risk of temporary suspension. In particular, Jordan's suspension was being discussed by the leadership team: his bad behaviour was considered among the worst.

(New paragraph)

However, the greater issue at play was that none of the teachers in the science department could control the students. The headteacher has been reminded that teaching isn't purely about knowledge and the ability to put new ideas across; it's equally important to be able to earn the respect of the class, and respect them in return. A strong, mutual agreement between a teacher and their students is vital for success in lessons.

Mrs Brown reassured staff and parents that further training would take place to make sure teachers were able to handle the more excitable and troublesome classes: "Making sure that the school is a safe and efficient environment for students and teachers is still a high priority."

2.

There were many complaints from students in the aftermath of changes to the school uniform. The changes to the uniform would be coming into effect in the next school year, but new uniform was rolled out to students who needed it at that moment. Any students who were representing the school at events (there weren't many external events at that point in the year) would be required to wear the new uniform.

(New paragraph)

The colour of the school tie had been changed from a deep blue to bright purple, with an emblem at the top. Moreover, the jumpers worn were made brighter, resulting in a clash of colours.

*(**New paragraph**)*

*Another less controversial change was to rules regarding shoes. **Up** until this point, the school had allowed dark brown shoes to be worn as well as black shoes; the intention being that it allowed for more freedom in choosing what to wear. However, the school had taken a hard-line stance against brown shoes, only allowing black school shoes to be worn. This would come into effect immediately.*

3.

According to the report given by witnesses on the school's playing field, the incident had taken place as follows:

*(**New paragraph**)*

1. *Henry had climbed the tree in the northwest corner of the field; (**New Line**)*

2. *Lalita and Nazeem spotted Henry and told him he should climb down before he got hurt; (**New Line**)*

3. *Henry shouted that Lalita and Nazeem were 'crybabies' and needed to grow up; (**New Line**)*

4. *Angered, Lalita and Nazeem threw twigs and stones at Henry until he lost his grip on the tree branch; (**New Line**)*

5. *Henry fell from the tree and sprained his ankle.*

Conclusion

As previously mentioned, the punctuation section of the literacy skills test contains more available marks than any of the others. It can also be a rather tricky section, since it requires an understanding of the aforementioned punctuation marks.

However, if you've used this chapter to learn each of the devices and their uses, you will be in a strong position to answer the questions in the punctuation section.

Once you feel confident about the contents of this chapter, move onto grammar. This will be covered in the next chapter.

THE QTS
LITERACY
SKILLS TEST
GRAMMAR

Introduction

Of all the aspects of literacy, grammar may be the most difficult to understand. There are a number of rules to remember and there are plenty of grammatical errors which people make on a day-to-day basis.

Grammar is essentially a set of rules and conventions which determine how language is structured. It is concerned with sentence boundaries, nouns, prepositions, and other devices and kinds of words. These may seem daunting at first, but in this chapter you will learn the grammatical rules which are likely to show up in the literacy skills test.

Unlike punctuation, which is somewhat determined by preference and style, grammar is usually either correct or incorrect. In other words, you can be right or wrong about your sentence structure, use of nouns/pronouns, or in your use of 'should have' and 'should of'. While you can get away with never using a semi-colon, you will need to know all of the grammatical devices at play, because almost all of them will appear in your reading and writing.

Grammar is important to a teacher for a number of reasons. Firstly, good grammar skills allow you to write in a way which is free from ambiguity. Poor grammar can lead to confusing sentences and whole passages which don't make sense.

As a teacher, you will need to be able to write material which students and colleagues can read. A firm grasp on grammatical conventions and how they work is vital, because this will allow you to present your ideas effectively. More importantly, you may need to help students with passages which have been written poorly, or correct poor grammar on their part.

In this chapter, you will learn the important features of grammar, which might appear in the literacy skills test.

What is the grammar section like?

Depending on the test you sit, there could be between 10 and 12 marks available for the grammar section. You will be tested on your ability to understand written English and how to use it.

In this section of the literacy skills test, you will be presented with either two or three short passages. These texts will have gaps missing, and you will need to choose from one of four choices to fill the gaps in. The choice you make must be grammatically correct in order to receive marks.

Some questions may ask you to examine four sentences, and then choose the one which best meets a given convention. For example, a question may ask you to look at four sentences and decide which one best follows rules regarding sentence boundaries. Alternatively, you may just be asked to pick whichever is generally more grammatically correct.

This section of the literacy skills test is usually divided into multiple exercises. All this really means for you is that the subject matter of the questions will change throughout this section. Your task will remain the same.

Grammatical Devices

The following sections will outline the key elements of grammar that you will need to know in order to perform well in this section. These have been divided into three main sections:

* Standard English Conventions;

* Grammatical Clarity;

* Professionalism.

It is worth remembering that the test will not have enough questions to assess every aspect of grammar mentioned in this chapter. However, it is important that you take the time to learn them all equally, since you have no way of accurately predicting which grammatical items will appear.

Standard English Conventions

Articles of grammar which fall under this category are associated with the conventions of the English language, and form what is known as "Standard English." They mostly involve poorly structured or fragmented sentences, incorrect use of nouns/pronouns, and a general lack of cohesion.

Sentence Boundaries

Many native and non-native English speakers struggle with creating sentences of an appropriate length. This is often the result of confusion over where full stops should be placed.

If you have jumped into this chapter first, it is strongly recommended that you read the punctuation chapter beforehand, since elements of grammar such as sentence boundaries can be impacted by one's understanding of punctuation. In particular, make sure that you read the sections on full stops and commas. Once you feel comfortable with their usages, return to this section.

The longer a sentence goes on for, the more likely it is to become convoluted and difficult to read. For the sake of clarity, shorter sentences are often preferable over longer ones, since they prevent a text from becoming unwieldy.

To picture this better, think of a text as a head of hair, with each single hair representing a sentence. As hair grows, individual hairs are more likely to become knotted and tangled with one another, making it difficult for the entire head of hair to be tamed. However, shorter hair can be looked after more easily and is less likely to become tangled and knotted.

Passages are similar, in that lots of long sentences will be hard for many people to understand. Therefore, you should try to make sentences as short as possible. While a variety of longer and shorter sentences can make a piece of writing more interesting to read, you shouldn't be too adventurous with your sentence length until you have a firm grasp of sentence boundaries. Sentences which run on for too long do not look professional or intelligent – they are often cumbersome and confusing to the reader.

Here's an example of a sentence which has poor boundaries:

> *There wasn't a clear explanation as to why the guest speakers had to cancel at the last minute, it could have been the case that they were ill, but they should have given some reason for their absence.*

This sentence has incorrect boundaries as it is combining two main clauses. It should read like this:

> *There wasn't a clear explanation as to why the guest speakers had to cancel at the last minute. It could have been the case that they were ill, but they should have given some reason for their absence.*

The incorrect example has enough content for two sentences, and therefore a full stop should be placed after the phrase 'last minute'.

Poor sentence boundaries usually occur when the writer misuses commas or misunderstands the main clause of a sentence. In this instance, it is appropriate to add a full stop, although a semi-colon may have been acceptable as well. However, it is best to use a full stop rather than a semi-colon if you are not confident in your writing abilities. Shorter sentences are usually a much safer bet than longer sentences.

Fragmented Sentences

While poor sentence boundaries occur when a sentence is too long, a fragment is what occurs when a sentence is too short. Fragments usually emerge accidentally while writing, when what should be part of a sentence receives a full stop too early, resulting in a fragment of a sentence being left over. Here is an example of a fragmented sentence:

> *While they should have given some reason for their absence.*

This is a sentence fragment because the use of 'while' suggests that more information was to be given:

> *While they should have given some reason for their absence, accidents happen and the organisers may have simply forgotten to let us know.*

Although sentences are hard to define, fragments usually occur when a sentence lacks at least one of two necessary components: a subject and a verb. Here is an example of a sentence with a subject but no verb.

> *The main source of energy for your body.*

This sentence doesn't contain a verb and is therefore a fragment. It can be fixed by adding a verb:

> *Carbohydrates are the main source of energy for your body.*

By adding the verb 'are', the fragment has become a fully-fledged sentence.

Bear in mind that not all fragments lack a subject and/or a verb. Sometimes, as shown in the first example, the sentence has clearly been cut off too early. However, it is useful to try and find the subject and the verb in a sentence to tell whether it is a fragment or not.

Cohesion

Cohesion is concerned with how sentences link together. Up until this point, you have learned about how to make a sentence internally consistent by adhering to sentence boundaries.

However, the boundaries of grammar do not end at individual sentences. Whole passages need to make sense, which means that sentences need to co-operate with one another. The aim of cohesion is to make sure that sentences connect and flow well.

One way in which a lack of cohesion can occur across sentences is through confusion of pronouns. This is particularly the case when singulars and plurals are confused, resulting in ambiguity.

<u>Here's an example of a sentence which misuses pronouns:</u>

> *There was one person left in the hall. They should be able to lock up on their own.*

The problem with this sentence is that the word 'person' is a singular phrase, while 'they' is a plural pronoun. However, since the gender of the individual isn't confirmed to be male or female, the pronouns 'he' or 'she' aren't appropriate. However, the sentence could be re-written to avoid the pronoun altogether:

> *The one person left in the hall should be able to lock up alone.*

By rewriting the sentence, the pronoun is avoided and the same meaning is preserved.

Another way in which a passage can lack cohesion is through the misuse of cohesive devices. These are words or phrases which act as connectives between sentences, setting the tone. Previously, we have referred to these as sentence adverbs. Words of this kind include:

However	For example	Additionally	Furthermore
In contrast	Therefore	Consequently	In other words
Conversely	Overall	In comparison	Regardless
Similarly	Likewise	Equally	Moreover

When using these cohesive devices, make sure that they match the tone of the sentence that they are followed by.

<u>Here is an example of a sentence which misuses a sentence adverb:</u>

> *The changes to the seating arrangement were well-received. However, the students were performing better than ever.*

The use of the word 'however' is inappropriate because the two sentences do not show conflicting information. 'However' is a contrasting cohesive device – used to connect two sentences that show contradiction or conflict, such as:

> The changes to the seating arrangement were well-received. However, students were misbehaving more than ever.

In this case, the content of the first sentence conflicts with the content of the second. Therefore, the word 'however' is suitable.

With regards to the initial example, another sentence adverb would need to be used, such as:

> The changes to the seating arrangement were well-received. Additionally, the students were performing better than ever.

Since the two statements support each other, the second sentence is building on top of the information in the first. For this reason, 'additionally' is suitable since it is a sentence adverb which demonstrates reinforcement of an idea.

In order to make sure your use of sentence adverbs is correct, you will need to know the general categories that the phrases fall into.

Here are some examples to get you started:

Listing	First/Firstly	Furthermore	Next	Finally	Moreover
Reinforcement	Furthermore	Moreover	In addition	Also	Besides
Contrast	Conversely	In comparison	In contrast	Instead	On the contrary
Similarity	Similarly	Likewise	Equally	In the same way	In a similar sense
Summary	To conclude	To summarise	Overall	In conclusion	Therefore
Highlighting	In particular	Particularly	Especially	Mainly	

You may notice that some of these words belong in more than one category. Words such as 'furthermore' can be used in a number of contexts.

Disagreement between Subject and Verb

This is a form of cross-sentence incoherence which is the result of incorrect tense or singularity/plurality. This section will cover the ways in which this grammatical error can appear.

The first error occurs when two or more nouns are matched with a singular verb (e.g. 'was,' 'is'):

Gemma and Nazeem was the only people left in the hall.

This is an error because the two nouns form a group, and therefore need a plural:

*Gemma and Nazeem **were** the only people left in the hall.*

If the subject is a plural (i.e. two or more nouns grouped together) then the verb needs to be plural as well.

The second error appears when a plural determiner (e.g. 'some,' 'all,' 'less') is paired with a singular verb (e.g. 'was,' 'is'):

Fewer people has arrived on time than usual.

The determiner 'fewer' is a plural, and 'has' is a singular verb. The verb needs to be changed to a plural:

*Fewer people **have** arrived on time than usual.*

If the determiner is a plural, then the verb must also be a plural.

The next grammatical error is the opposite: when the determiner of the sentence is singular and the plural is a verb. The same rule applies – both need to be of the same kind:

This lesson were successful in conveying its key points.

This should read as:

*This lesson **was** successful in conveying its key points.*

Generally speaking, it's important that plurals match plurals and singulars match singulars. Keep an eye out for which appears in a sentence and then make sure every determiner matches it correctly.

Determiners

Determiners are words which signify the context of the words which follow them. Determiners are a large category of words, which can be separated into two groups: specific and general determiners.

Specific determiners include possessives:

My	Your	His	Her	Whose

They also include demonstratives:

That	These	Those	This

Specific determiners also include the definite article ('the') and interrogatives such as 'which'.

The general determiners include:

A	An	Other	What

Correct use of demonstratives is particularly important and people often confuse them.

For example:

> *Standing in the corridor was that teacher.*

Should read:

> *Standing in the corridor was **the** teacher.*

This determiner is appropriate because 'that' refers to something earlier in the text. Since the teacher in question has not been referred to yet in the text, 'that' is not referring to anything previously mentioned.

Determiner/Noun Errors

This grammatical error occurs when the type of determiner does not match the noun of the sentence. For instance, if the noun or noun phrase is plural (e.g. 'cats' or 'type of car') then the determiner must be plural as well:

> *Those type of cars is incredibly reliable.*

This should read as:

> *Those type of cars **are** incredibly reliable.*

To understand this better, we need to deconstruct the phrase:

Determiner	Noun/Noun Phrase	Verb
Those	Type of cars	are

The noun phrase contains a headword: the main part of the phrase. In this case, 'cars' is the headword. For these sentences, the singularity/plurality of the determiner and verb must match that of the headword. Since 'cars' is plural, the determiner and verb must also be plural. Therefore, the verb 'are' is correct while 'is' is incorrect. Likewise, the determiner 'those' is correct, while 'that' and 'this' would be incorrect.

Should have/Should of

This is an incredibly common grammatical error which people make in their everyday lives. The way we speak is partially to blame: we often pronounce the 'have' of 'should have' as a 've'. However, this often sounds like we are saying 'of', which is grammatically incorrect.

> *I should of gone to the meeting early to speak with the project leader.*

This should read as:

> *I should **have** gone to the meeting early to speak with the project leader.*

In a less formal context, it might be appropriate to use the contraction of 'should have': 'should've'.

> *I **should've** gone to the meeting early to speak with the project leader.*

This applies to many more of the modal verbs in the English language, such as:

      Could   *Would*   *Must*

It is important to remember that 'of' never follows these words. If it sounds as though an 'of' is being added, it is mostly likely the word 'have', which may be contracted to 've' such as 'could've', 'would've' and 'must've'.

The sounds which we make in spoken English can be deceptive, and the have/ of confusion highlights this. When we speak, we naturally make contractions that we know other English speakers will understand. This is often done for the sake of briefness – it's easier and quicker to say 'could've' than 'could have'. Eventually, the 've' sound starts to sound like an 'of' sound, resulting in bad grammatical habits when writing. Remember that the sounds made in spoken English don't always match those in standard written English.

Inappropriate Verb Forms

This grammatical error occurs when the verb and the words around it are not formed properly, or in some cases do not appear at all. This is an easy mistake to make when writing, so pay close attention to your verb forms.

> *Some of the ex-students managed stop by during their university summer holidays to say hello.*

The verb form of the above sentence is missing. It should read:

> *Some of the ex-students managed **to** stop by during their university summer holidays to say hello.*

In this sentence, the main verb is 'managed', and it requires the verb form 'to' in order to make sense. Likewise, the same sentence could be missing another verb form:

> *Some of the ex-students managed to stop during their university summer holidays to say hello.*

This should read as:

> *Some of the ex-students managed to stop **by** during their university summer holidays to say hello.*

Sometimes, the verb form might be present but incorrect. For example:

> *Some of the ex-students managed to stop to during their university summer holidays to say hello.*

The word 'to' after the verb 'stop' is an incorrect verb form. You can 'stop in', 'stop at' and 'stop by', but you can't 'stop to'. The best way to discover the appropriate verb form for each verb is to listen to people speaking. In particular, it might be useful to listen to how people speak in scripted radio and television shows, since they will use the correct grammar unless it's for effect. However, be wary of American spoken English since it often omits verb forms:

> *'Go fetch the keys,' Mrs Brown demanded.*

In American English, this is structured normally, and is acceptable. However, the literacy skills test expects an understanding of Standard English, and therefore you must make sure not to omit verb forms:

> *'Go to fetch the keys,' Mrs Brown demanded.*

In addition to hearing people speak, reading will always reinforce your vocabulary and therefore your understanding of verb forms. Inappropriate or missing verb forms can be easily overlooked while writing, but their rules are generally straight forward.

Noun/Pronoun errors

Pronouns are words used in the place of a noun. Pronouns are used to make reference to nouns without having to reuse the name repeatedly:

> *John was having difficulties with his maths homework.*

Could become:

> *He was having difficulties with his maths homework.*

Both 'he' and 'his' in the above sentence are pronouns – they make reference to John. However, they are clearly two separate words. The type of pronoun changes depending on its role in the sentence:

He	John
Him	John
Himself	John
His	John's

While 'he', 'him' and 'himself' all directly refer to John, they do so in different ways:

> *It was John all along!*

Becomes:

> *It was **him** all along!*

> *John kept the last piece of cake for John* **(the same person).**

Becomes:

> *John kept the last piece of cake for **himself**.*

> *John felt that John could do the job better.*

Becomes:

> *John felt that **he** could do the job better.*

Finally, the term 'his' is used to demonstrate ownership:

> *John's homework was handed in on-time despite struggling with it.*

Becomes:

> ***His** homework was handed in on-time despite struggling with it.*

Depending on the noun, the pronouns will behave differently:

> *Katie had no problem with Katie's homework.*

Becomes:

> *Katie had no problem with **her** homework.*

'Her' demonstrates ownership for female nouns, but also works in the same way as 'him' does for male nouns:

> *It was Katie all along!*

Becomes:

> *It was **her** all along!*

This table shows the major pronouns for each kind of noun:

I	You	She	He	It	We	They
Me	You	Her	Him	It	Us	Them
My	Your	Her	His	Its	Our	Their
Mine	Yours	Hers	His	Its	Ours	Theirs
Myself	Yourself	Herself	Himself	Itself	Ourselves	Themselves

Keep this table in mind when tackling questions where the nouns and pronouns have been confused:

Those shoes are my.

This should read as:

*Those shoes are **mine**.*

The final problem involving nouns and pronouns occurs when there is confusion between using 'me' or 'I':

My friends and me stayed at the restaurant until it closed.

Should read as:

My friends and I stayed at the restaurant until it closed.

However, there are some cases where 'me' is appropriate, such as:

A member of staff escorted my friends and me to the head teacher's office.

When dealing with these cases, try and remove other parties in the sentence (e.g. 'my friends') and see whether 'me' or 'I' is more appropriate:

> *I stayed at the restaurant until it closed.*

> *A member of staff escorted me to the head teacher's office.*

Generally speaking, whichever pronoun is suitable without the additional parties is suitable with them as well.

Comparatives and Superlatives

Comparatives are kinds of adjectives which allow us to make comparisons with two kinds of object. For example:

> *Henry's use of punctuation was **sloppier** than that of his classmates.*

'Sloppier' is the comparative in this sentence, and it is being used to demonstrate a difference between Henry's use of punctuation and the punctuation of his classmates. The word 'sloppy' is turned into a comparative by removing the 'y' and adding an 'ier' to the end of the adjective.

Another way to create a comparative is to add 'more' as a prefix (e.g. 'more acceptable'). This is used for words in which adding an 'er' would make no sense. For example, turning 'acceptable' into 'acceptable-er' does not look right, and does not represent spoken or written English.

Likewise, if an adjective can be turned into a comparative by adding 'er' to the end (e.g. 'sloppier', 'happier', 'closer' or 'newer') then it is grammatically incorrect to use 'more' instead:

> *The interactive boards in the ICT classrooms were more new than those in the English department.*

This should read as:

> *The interactive boards in the ICT classrooms were **newer** than those in the English department.*

The best way to learn which is appropriate is by reading more. By reading, you will become accustomed to whether 'er' or 'more' is suitable for turning an adjective into a comparative.

As well as comparatives, there are superlatives. These signify when an object is the most of a certain property as possible, or more than any other object in the context:

> *Henry's use of punctuation was the **sloppiest**.*

'Sloppiest' is the superlative of this sentence, and it demonstrates that the object/subject (Henry's use of punctuation) is the most sloppy it can be, or that it was more sloppy than everyone else's use of punctuation. Generally speaking, superlatives are reserved for when there are more than two subjects in the context. For example, if there are only two people in the context (Henry and Gemma), then the following is less grammatically appropriate:

> *Henry's use of punctuation was the sloppiest.*

Since the context only involves two people, a comparative should be used:

> *Henry's use of punctuation was **sloppier**.*

If there are more than two subjects (Henry, Gemma and Katie) then a superlative is necessary for the sake of clarity, since you would need to demonstrate that Henry's use of punctuation was sloppier than all of the other parties rather than just one other.

Incorrect Prepositions

Prepositions are words which signify where the associated object is in time and space. There's nothing science-fiction about this: prepositions describe where an object is and at what time. The following words are prepositions (bear in mind that there are many more):

At	Across	Above	Below
In	Out	Outside	Off
On	Among/Amongst	Alongside	Beneath
Within	Without	Beside	During

As previously mentioned, prepositions are important because they allow us to make statements about where something is:

> *There is a man **on** the roof.*

> *Nobody attends the optional sessions **during** lunchtime.*

These basic prepositions are quite easy to learn, but wider problems occur when complex prepositions are introduced. These include:

According to	Different to/from	Due to
Next to	Aside from	Apart from
As well as	Near to	Together with

Essentially, complex prepositions consist of two or more words. The confusion rises when deciding which words to include (e.g. 'to', 'than', 'from', 'with'). Most of these are actually quite intuitive and you will likely pick them up by reading, writing and listening to people speak. However, others can be confusing. For instance, 'different to' and 'different from' are both appropriate complex prepositions:

> *The answers given by the more attentive students were **different from** those of the others.*

> *The answers given by the more attentive students were **different to** those of the others.*

'Different than', on the other hand, is incorrect:

> *The answers given by the more attentive students were **different than** those of the others.*

For this kind of grammatical error, just be sure to remember that 'different than' is currently not an accepted preposition.

Relative Pronouns in Subordinate Clauses

This section will be focusing on subordinate clauses as well as what are known as 'relative pronouns'. If you remember from the sections on sentence boundaries and fragmented sentences, each sentence only has one main clause. However, subordinate clauses can be introduced to add more information or to make a sentence longer for the sake of variety. Subordinate clauses aren't always necessary and can quite often be circumvented by starting a new sentence. However, those with a stronger grasp of the English language will want to use longer sentences to make their writing more interesting.

Take this example of a sentence with and without an additional subordinate clause:

> *It is important to pay attention to a student's weaknesses.*

With a subordinate clause:

> *It is important to pay attention to a student's weaknesses in order to help them improve.*

A subordinate clause only makes sense if it is accompanied by a main clause.

A relative pronoun is a word or phrase which connects a subordinate clause to a main clause:

> *It is important to pay attention to a student's weaknesses **in order to** help them improve.*

In this case, the phrase 'in order to' acts as the connective between the main clause and the subordinate clause.

Relative pronouns include:

| Who | Whom | Which | That |

These are more subtle connectives than 'in order to' or 'because' and can be used as follows:

> *There was no one in the room **who** could answer the question as well as Gemma did.*

> *There was only one person in the room **that** could answer the question as well as Gemma could.*

Errors made with relative pronouns usually occur when the wrong pronoun is used. For example, 'which' is reserved for inanimate objects such as trees, cars, computers and buildings:

> *There was a car parked by the road who had been broken into.*

This should read as:

> *There was a car parked by the road **which** had been broken into.*

In contrast, the relative pronoun 'who' is used for people:

> *There was a student at the back of the classroom **who** had been talking for the entire lesson.*

The pronoun 'who' is often given to larger and more intelligent animals, particularly pets.

Relative Pronouns – Who and Whom

Another confusion with relative pronouns comes from the words 'who' and 'whom'. Many people do not know the difference, and will mostly just use 'who' even if 'whom' is grammatically correct.

The word 'whom' is used when referring to the object of a sentence. An object is a thing which is having something done to it:

> *Henry hugged Jacob.*

In this sentence, the object is Jacob because he is the one being hugged. Henry is the subject: he is the one doing the hugging.

'Whom' is correctly used in the following sentence:

> *Jacob, whom Henry hugged suddenly, was frozen to the spot.*

Whilst 'who' would be suitable in the following sentence:

> *Henry, who hugged Jacob suddenly, was awfully happy to have been invited to the party.*

Both of these sentences also use 'who' and 'whom' as relative pronouns, connecting subordinate clauses to the rest of the sentence.

Adverbial Forms

Adverbs (e.g. 'quickly', 'brashly', 'fast') are all used to describe a verb:

> *Lalita dived swiftly into the pool.*

In this sentence, 'swiftly' is the adverb. It is made by adding 'ly' to an adjective: 'swift'. However, not all adverbs end with an 'ly':

> *Nazeem drove straight despite poor visibility on the road.*

In this sentence, 'straight' is the adverb: it is adding description to the verb 'drove'. So, it is evident that there are adverbs which do not need an additional 'ly'. This can cause some people to miss the additional 'ly' where it is necessary, such as in this case:

> *Lalita dived swift into the pool.*

This should read as:

> *Lalita dived **swiftly** into the pool.*

When writing a piece of work, check your adverbs in case you've made this mistake.

Grammatical Clarity

The result of good literacy skills is clarity in writing. Grammar, spelling and punctuation all play a role in making a piece of writing easy to read and understand, but this section will tackle grammatical conventions which are principally concerned with clarity.

In the test, you will need to know when a piece of writing is clear. More importantly, you will need to know what to do if a piece of writing is not clear. Creating a clear text is almost always the priority when writing, since good ideas can only be fully effective if represented well.

Inconsistency in Past/Present/Future Tenses

Tenses are used to signify time. Specifically, tenses appear in the form of verbs:

Past	Present	Future
Ran	Runs	Will Run
Jumped	Jumps	Will Jump
Was	Am/Is	Will be

It is completely acceptable to have more than one tense in a single sentence:

Henry was in the toilet, but now he is in the classroom.

In this sentence, 'was' is the past tense verb, while 'is' acts as the present tense verb. An additional future tense can be added too:

Henry was in the toilet, is now in the classroom, and is going to be outside on the playground.

The future tense in this sentence is 'is going to be'.

It's now clear that multiple tenses in the same sentence are not an issue so long as they are clear. Issues with tenses occur when there is an inconsistency within a sentence:

> *Henry was running and overtakes into first place.*

This sentence is incorrect because there are two contradictory tenses at play. First, we are told that Henry 'was running' (past tense) and then that he 'overtakes' (present tense) into first place. The tense of the sentence had already been established as the past tense, and therefore the tense of the second verb must be changed:

> *Henry was running and **overtook** into first place.*

This makes more sense, since it implied that while Henry was running, he overtook into first place. The previous sentence suggested that Henry was running, stopped running, and is now overtaking into first place.

The following sentence is also incorrect:

> *Henry was running and will overtake into first place.*

This implied that Henry was running, has now stopped running, but will somehow overtake into first place. This is entirely possible – perhaps there is a break mid-race in which Henry is currently stopping, and when the race restarts he will overtake into first place. However, the sentence does not make this clear: it appears as though the race has finished but in the future Henry will overtake into first place.

The sentence should read as:

> *Henry was running, **is currently stopping for a break**, but will overtake into first place.*

This extra clause fills the gap between the past tense verb and future tense verb, providing clarity to the sentence.

Ambiguous Pronouns

This occurs when a pronoun could refer to multiple different things in a sentence or a text:

> *The room was occupied with dogs of both genders, as well as a number of the students. While there were some concerns, they had been neutered so there shouldn't be any incidents.*

In the second sentence, the word 'they' has been used to refer to a group from the last sentence. However, there are two different groups which could be referred to: the dogs and the students. Obviously, it isn't the students who have been neutered, but the pronoun 'they' doesn't make that clear in the text. Potentially, someone could read the passage and believe that the students have been sterilised and not the dogs.

Overuse of nouns can look incredibly clumsy:

> *John went to the shop. John bought some crisps and then John walked to school. John arrived at school on-time despite the fact that John had left later than usual.*

However, sometimes it is better to reuse the noun in order to avoid a misunderstanding in the text:

> *The room was occupied with dogs of both genders, as well as a number of the students. While there were some concerns, **the dogs** had been neutered so there weren't any incidents.*

By reusing the noun instead of using the pronoun 'they', it has been made clear that the dogs were the group which had been neutered, not the students.

Attachment

Attachment occurs when a piece of information is added to a sentence, specifically to a certain subject. However, ambiguity can arise if it isn't clear what the additional information is being attached to:

> *We have all attended a meeting about the observation this afternoon.*

What is or has occurred this afternoon? Is it the meeting about the observation, the observation itself, or neither? The sentence does not seem to give an answer either way.

If the meeting occurred this afternoon, the sentence should be structured as follows:

> *This afternoon, we all attended a meeting about the observation.*

By placing 'this afternoon' at the start of the sentence, it is implied that the meeting occurred this afternoon. The time of the observation is still unknown.

If the observation is occurring this afternoon, then the sentence needs to be restructured:

> *There is an observation this afternoon; we have all attended a meeting about it.*

A slightly more cumbersome (but still clear) way of structuring the sentence is:

> *We have all attended a meeting about the observation which will be occurring this afternoon.*

The use of the future tense 'will be' shows that the observation is happening after the meeting, which implies that it occurs in the afternoon.

Confusion of Words

There are many words in the English language which sound very similar, and without proper explanation you might believe that they mean the same thing. In the worst case scenario, you may even be using two different words interchangeably without realising it. This section will tackle some of the major confusions of words that people face in their daily lives, and that you may face as a teacher.

The first pair of words that are easily confused are 'stationary' and 'stationery'. Despite only being different by a single letter, these words have almost entirely different meanings:

'Stationary' is an adjective which describes something as not moving:

*The train was now **stationary** as there was a cow standing on the track.*

'Stationery' is a noun. Pens, pencils, rulers and other writing materials come under the category of 'stationery':

*There was **stationery** scattered across the floor as the students decided to climb across the desk.*

In many cases, someone with an understanding of the two words will still be able to make sense of your writing. However, it's vital that you understand the difference yourself if you want to be a teacher.

Another incredibly common confusion is found in the difference between 'affect' and 'effect'. The easiest way to remember the difference is to bear in mind that 'effect' is almost always a noun:

*Threats of suspension seem to have no **effect** on the troublesome students.*

'Affect', on the other hand, is used as a verb:

*Threats of suspension significantly **affected** the students who were usually very well-behaved.*

People are often confused between 'infer' and 'imply'. These two cannot be used interchangeably as they mean very different things, although they are related.

To infer something, or to make an inference, is to glean something or come to a conclusion from a piece of information:

*The teacher **inferred** that many of the students had not completed their homework by the way they remained silent when questions were asked.*

In contrast, to imply something is to suggest something. In addition, an implication is a potential result of something:

*The way that the students avoided questions during the lesson **implied** that they had not done their homework.*

Generally speaking, 'imply' is a lot more passive than 'infer'. People actively make an inference from some information, whilst implying something can occur without intending it.

There are many more words which people get confused by, and learning the differences can only be done with practice. Here are a selection of more words which are often confused – take the time to learn the differences between them:

Accept/Except	Advice/Advise
Allowed/Aloud	Amoral/Immoral
Bare/Bear	Coarse/Course
Discrete/Discreet	Elicit/Illicit
Pour/Pore	Tortuous/Torturous

Story/Storey	Picture/Pitcher
Principle/Principal	Meter/Metre
Envelop/Envelope	Ensure/Insure

Participles

Participles are modified verbs which act as adjectives:

Verb	Participle	Participle in context
Boil	Boiled	The boiled egg...
Burn	Burnt	The burnt toast...

These are examples of past participles. A past participle can be used in a sentence as follows:

She presented some toast which was burnt by the oven.

In this sentence, 'burnt' describes the toast. Participles do not have a subject, and they always appear after a verb such as 'to be'.

Participles become an issue when they are unrelated. This occurs when it isn't clear who or what the participle is relating to:

Working alongside one another, the task was completed on time.

In this sentence, 'working' acts as a participle. However, it is not related to any subjects. This can be corrected by rewriting the sentence:

Working alongside one another, Katie and Jordan completed the task on time.

Here, the participle is now related to two subjects: Katie and Jordan.

Professionalism

In the chapter on comprehension, professionalism and style will be discussed in the context of writing to a particular audience, or figuring out the target audience of a text. This section will cover conventions which add to the professionalism of a piece. While the errors listed in this section may not make a text unreadable due to ambiguity, they need to be avoided in order to make a piece of writing look professional.

Tautologies

Tautologies occur when redundant words are added to a sentence:

> It is an **_actual fact_** that students who have a short break after an hour of learning will be refreshed for the second hour.

'Actual fact' is a redundant phrase because all facts are actual. Part of the definition of 'fact' is actuality (i.e. it is true) and so 'actual fact' means something along the lines of "an actual statement about the world which is actual." The repetition of 'actual' means that it is redundant. The sentence should read as:

> It is a **_fact_** that students who have a short break after an hour of learning will be refreshed for the second hour.

There are plenty of redundancies made in everyday language. Here are some examples:

False pretence	Added bonus	Each and every	Forever and ever
Major breakthrough	Written down	Suddenly exploded	Repeat again
Close proximity	End result	Plan ahead	Completely finished

Tautologies often occur when using acronyms. For example:

> *The fire alarm will sound at 9:00 a.m. in the morning.*

In this case, 'in the morning' is redundant since 'a.m.' refers to the morning.

Inconsistent Tone

Inconsistency in tone occurs when a text moves between a formal and informal tone. Not all writing is – or should be – in a formal tone. In particular, works of fiction benefit from an informal tone, which help to display a character's current frame of mind or overall personality. For example, many characters in William Shakespeare's plays who belonged to a lower social class would have their dialogue written in prose and would be presented as more informal. In contrast, characters of higher status would generally be more poetic in their speech. So, it's clear that a change of tone can be acceptable if used for literary impact.

In contrast, non-fiction texts benefit from adhering to one tone throughout. In most cases, a formal tone is preferable. This is because formal language and a lack of regional dialect or slang will be easier to read, for a broader range of people. When writing, it is important that your tone is consistent. Sometimes, you might need to write a piece which adopts an informal tone, to make it more accessible to younger people. Generally you will want to take a formal tone in your writing.

As previously mentioned, slang and colloquialisms can often cause inconsistency in tone:

> *There were concerns that new rules on uniform would drive some students* ***absolutely mental****.*

The final phrase of this sentence does not fit the overall tone. Instead, the sentence should be re-worded to read:

> *There were concerns that new rules on uniform would make some of the students **extremely angry**.*

The tone has now shifted to be more formal.

An inconsistency in tone can also occur when the words 'you' and 'one' are used interchangeably in a sentence:

> *Although **one** may think that the tone of their work is consistent, **you** should check your work, to make sure you haven't accidentally slipped into an inconsistent tone.*

In this sentence, both 'one' and 'you' have been used interchangeably. While these two words can be used in the same way, using both in the same sentence looks untidy. Preferably, you should choose one of them and use it consistently throughout the entire text:

> *Although **you** may think that the tone of your work is consistent, **you** should check your work to make sure you haven't accidentally slipped into an inconsistent tone.*

Or:

> *Although **one** may think that the tone of their work is consistent, **one** should check their work to make sure they haven't accidentally slipped into an inconsistent tone.*

Both of these amendments are acceptable, since they create a consistent tone.

Also bear in mind that these pronouns are directed at different bodies. 'I' is a first person pronoun, whilst 'you' is usually a second person pronoun. 'You' should be used when addressing the reader, while 'one' is a more general pronoun for addressing the third person.

At school you may have been taught that referring to yourself (with the 'I' pronoun or otherwise) in a piece of formal text is unacceptable:

> *I have come to the conclusion that the new rules regarding uniform are unfair on the students.*

In the real world, the acceptability of using 'I' in a formal piece of text changes. Some institutions may condemn it outright, whilst others will accept its use where appropriate. For the sake of the literacy skills test, assume that referring to yourself is less preferable than using 'one' or 'you'. However, in everyday life you should look to the conventions that your employer and colleagues use.

The final occurrence of tonal inconsistency which will be covered in this section regards the use of active and passive forms in a sentence:

> *A large number of people **queued** for the food and then it **was eaten**.*

This sentence uses both passive and active verbs. The active verb is 'queued' while the passive is 'was eaten'. This can be corrected as follows:

> *A large number of people **queued** for the food and then **ate** it.*

In this revised sentence, both are active.

Excessive Sentence Length

As mentioned earlier in this chapter, longer sentences can be a problem for less experienced writers. A writer with a strong grasp of sentence boundaries and punctuation will have little difficulty when constructing longer sentences, but the less knowledgeable run the risk of creating sentences which are far too long. This is an issue because it makes a text harder to follow.

Naturally, people use punctuation such as full stops and commas to pause while reading. This may only be for a slight moment, but it allows for the reader to collect their thoughts about the sentence or clause that they have just read. The longer a sentence is, the more there is for a reader to digest once they reach a good point to pause. A good writer will adhere to sentence boundaries and make sure that there are plenty of points for a reader to pause at, but less experienced writers might create sentences which are awfully clumsy:

> *So far seventeen students have been placed under observation with at least five of them at risk of temporary suspension particularly Jordan whose suspension was being discussed by the leadership team since his bad behaviour was considered among the worst.*

Quite often, these excessively long sentences can be broken into multiple sentences:

> *So far, seventeen students have been placed under observation, with at least five of them at risk of temporary suspension. In particular, Jordan's suspension was being discussed by the leadership team. His bad behaviour was considered among the worst.*

In the above example, both commas and full stops were used to create natural pause points for the reader. This way they know when to stop to digest the information that they are reading.

It's easy to get carried away when writing. When you're in the flow of writing and feel as though you have plenty to say, it's tempting to keep writing rather than stop to take stock of what you've written. Whenever you finish a paragraph, make sure to read back as if you were an ordinary reader and not the writer of the passage. If there is far too much in one sentence, it is best to break the text up into smaller sentences. One great way to check your sentences is to read them out loud. If you find yourself struggling for breath, or to finish the whole thing, then that's a good indication that your sentence is missing key pieces of punctuation.

In the test, bear in mind the rules about sentence boundaries and cohesion. In addition, it may be useful to revise full stops, commas, colons and semi-colons to make sure you are equipped to recognise a long, unwieldy sentence in the text.

Non-Parallelism

Non-parallelism occurs when lists are structured incorrectly. To best understand this problem, imagine the introduction to a list as the first half of a sentence, with each item in the list individually forming the second half:

> *In the next piece of writing, you must include:*
> - *An example of a semi-colon used correctly;*
> - *The correct spelling of a word with a double consonant.*

Each of the items, when combined with the introduction, should form a proper sentence:

> *In the next piece of writing, you must include an example of a semi-colon used correctly.*

> *In the next piece of writing, you must include the correct spelling of a word with a double consonant.*

Non-parallelism occurs when the items in the list do not form a proper sentence when combined with the introduction:

> *In the next piece of writing, you must include:*
> - *Include an example of a semi-colon used correctly;*
> - *Correct spelling of a word with a double consonant.*

If these items are connected to the introduction, they do not make sense:

> *In the next piece of writing, you must **include include** an example of a semi-colon used correctly.*

This repetition means that the sentence does not make sense. Therefore, 'include' should not be written in the item of the list, as shown in the first example.

> *In the next piece of writing, you must **include correct** spelling of a word with a double consonant.*

This sentence makes no sense because the word 'the' is missing after the word 'include' and before the word 'correct'. Therefore, 'the' must be added to the start of the item, as shown in the first example.

By thinking of the introduction and the item combining to make a sentence, you should be able to spot non-parallelism in a list. Whenever you come across a list either in the test or in your own writing, make sure to read them as full sentences in order to make sure that they are grammatically correct.

Grammar Tips

Grammar is an incredibly exhaustive field, so there aren't too many general tips to give. Remember that spoken English, while very efficient at making conversation and speaking in everyday life, doesn't accurately represent Standard English in a lot of cases. Therefore, be careful when practising for the test; try to block out thoughts about how sentences would be constructed when speaking.

Also remember that not every grammatical error will appear in the test. However, you should give as much attention to each grammatical convention as possible in order to make sure you aren't caught off-guard. Essentially, it pays to be prepared for anything to appear in the test.

Grammar – Sample Questions

Take a look at the following sample questions to get an idea of how the grammar section of the literacy skills test will appear and feel. Once you've looked through them, attempt answering them without looking at your notes. When you have finished answering the questions, take a look at the next section for answers and explanations. Use the explanations to improve on the types of question that you struggle with the most.

Sentence Boundaries

For this question, circle the option which best adheres to sentence boundaries.

So far, seventeen students have been placed under observation, with at least five of them at risk of temporary suspension…

_____

_____

A. *In particular, Jordan's suspension was being discussed by the leadership team: his bad behaviour was considered among the worst. It was quite likely that Jordan would face suspension, and possibly even permanent exclusion.*

B. *In particular Jordan's suspension was being discussed by the leadership team because his bad behaviour was considered among the worst and it was quite likely that Jordan would face suspension and possibly even permanent exclusion.*

C. *In particular, Jordan's suspension was being discussed by the leadership team: his bad behaviour was considered among the worst and it was quite likely that Jordan would face suspension, and possibly even permanent exclusion.*

D. *In particular, Jordan's suspension was being discussed by the leadership team: his bad behaviour was considered among the worst. It was quite likely that Jordan would face suspension and possibly even permanent exclusion.*

Inconsistency in Past/Present/Future Tenses

For this question, circle the option which has the most coherent use of different tenses.

There were a number of teachers who were...

_____

_____

A. *prepare to accompany the class on the school trip on the condition that they would not have to supervise the students alone.*

B. *prepared to accompany the class on the school trip on the condition that they would not have to supervise the students alone.*

C. *prepared to accompanied the class on the school trip on the condition that they did not have to supervise the students alone.*

D. *prepare to accompanied the class on the school trip on the condition that they would not have to supervise the students alone.*

Disagreement between Subject and Verb

For this question, circle the option in which the verb and the subject best suit one another.

Henry and Katie...

_____

_____

A. *was ready to work from the second that they entered the room. The rest of the group was struggling to organise themselves. The teacher weren't impressed by the chaos.*

B. *were ready to work from the second that they entered the room. The rest of the group were struggling to organise themselves. The teacher wasn't impressed by the chaos.*

C. *were ready to work from the second that they entered the room. The rest of the group was struggling to organise themselves. The teacher weren't impressed by the chaos.*

D. *was ready to work from the second that they entered the room. The rest of the group was struggling to organise themselves. The teacher wasn't impressed by the chaos.*

Cohesion

For this question, circle the option which makes best use of cohesive devices...

There were concerns that students were no longer taking PSHE lessons seriously.

_____

_____

A. *However, the students were annoyed that PSHE had taken from one of their hours of PE.*

B. *Conversely, the students were annoyed that PSHE had taken from one of their hours of PE.*

C. *Moreover, the students were annoyed that PSHE had taken from one of their hours of PE.*

D. *In other words, the students were annoyed that PSHE had taken from one of their hours of PE.*

Grammar – Answers and Explanations

Once you have answered the sample questions for this chapter, read these answers and explanations to see where you may have gone wrong, and how you can correct your mistakes.

Sentence Boundaries

So far, seventeen students have been placed under observation, with at least five of them at risk of temporary suspension.

A. **In particular, Jordan's suspension was being discussed by the leadership team: his bad behaviour was considered among the worst. It was quite likely that Jordan would face suspension, and possibly even permanent exclusion.**

B. *In particular Jordan's suspension was being discussed by the leadership team because his bad behaviour was considered among the worst and it was quite likely that Jordan would face suspension and possibly even permanent exclusion.*

C. *In particular, Jordan's suspension was being discussed by the leadership team: his bad behaviour was considered among the worst and it was quite likely that Jordan would face suspension, and possibly even permanent exclusion.*

D. *In particular, Jordan's suspension was being discussed by the leadership team: his bad behaviour was considered among the worst it was quite likely that Jordan would face suspension and possibly even permanent exclusion.*

The correct answer for this question is A. This is because all of its sentences contain no more than one main clause. In addition, the sentence makes use of punctuation marks such as colons and commas in order to separate the subordinate clauses from the main clauses.

The other answers do not make use of full stops, commas or colons to separate their clauses. More importantly, these options overuse the word 'and' in order to join clauses together, resulting in unwieldy sentences.

Inconsistency in Past/Present/Future Tenses

There were a number of teachers who were

A. *prepare to accompany the class on the school trip on the condition that they would not have to supervise the students alone.*

B. **prepared to accompany the class on the school trip on the condition that they would not have to supervise the students alone.**

C. *prepared to accompanied the class on the school trip on the condition that they will not have to supervise the students alone.*

D. *prepare to accompanied the class on the school trip on the condition that they will not have to supervise the students alone.*

The correct answer for this question is B. This is because the former part of the sentence ('There were a number of teachers who were') is in the past tense, and therefore the word 'prepare' needs to be modified to the past tense verb 'prepared'. Additionally, the word 'accompany' remains in the present tense, because it is connected to the past tense verb 'prepared'. Finally, 'would not' is the correct tense since it is hypothetical: the teachers accompanying and supervising is conditional on the fact that they would not have to do it on their own.

Answers A, C and D all make some of the mistakes listed above, and therefore are not satisfactory.

Disagreement between Subject and Verb

Henry and Katie

A. *was ready to work from the second that they entered the room. The rest of the group was struggling to organise themselves. The teacher weren't impressed by the chaos.*

B. **were ready to work from the second that they entered the room. The rest of the group were struggling to organise themselves. The teacher wasn't impressed by the chaos.**

C. *were ready to work from the second that they entered the room. The rest of the group was struggling to organise themselves. The teacher weren't impressed by the chaos.*

D. *was ready to work from the second that they entered the room. The rest of the group was struggling to organise themselves. The teacher wasn't impressed by the chaos.*

The correct answer to this question is B. Since Henry and Katie are a plural together, the correct verb is 'were'. The second error comes after the word 'group' – this should be 'were' since certain members of the group ('the rest') are being singled out. However, had this read as 'The group ___ struggling to organise themselves', then the correct verb would be 'was' since the group is being referred to as a single entity. Finally, the correct verb for the teacher in this case is 'wasn't'.

Cohesion

There were concerns that students were no longer taking PSHE lessons seriously.

A. *However, the students were annoyed that PSHE had taken from one of their hours of PE.*

B. *Conversely, the students were annoyed that PSHE had taken from one of their hours of PE.*

C. **Moreover, the students were annoyed that PSHE had taken from one of their hours of PE.**

D. *In other words, the students were annoyed that PSHE had taken from one of their hours of PE.*

The correct answer for this question is C. This is because of the tone of the introductory sentence in relation to the options in the answers. In the question, it is made clear that students were reacting negatively towards the PSHE lessons. The sentence in the answers (*'the students were annoyed that PSHE had taken from one of their hours of PE'*) also implies a negative reaction towards the lessons. Therefore, the only cohesive device which would be suitable for this passage is one which suggests reinforcement of an earlier point.

Both 'however' and 'conversely' are cohesive devices which demonstrate a contrast or contradiction and so answers A and B are unsatisfactory. The phrase 'in other words' acts as a cohesive device which reformulates the subject matter of the previous sentence. While this is more suitable than answers A and B, answer C is preferable since it contains a cohesive device which reinforces an earlier point: 'moreover'.

Conclusion

Grammar is a huge field, and encompasses so many different conventions that it may feel impossible to learn them all. However, if you use this chapter as well as the sample questions, you will be in a strong position to tackle the grammar section of the test.

Once you feel confident with the grammatical conventions discussed, move onto the next chapter.

THE QTS
LITERACY
SKILLS TEST
COMPREHENSION

Introduction

Unlike the rest of the test, which focuses mostly on your writing skills, the comprehension section evaluates your ability to read a piece of text and make assessments.

Reading is an essential part of being a teacher, regardless of your specialism. Modern teachers are often expected to read material which does not relate to their subject, but rather to teaching as a whole. School reports, government documents and other texts regarding education are often read by teachers. Some of this reading may be quite demanding, and might require a critical eye in order to identify key details.

In addition to this, teachers need good reading skills in order to work with a class of students. Good comprehension skills will allow you to quickly read a piece of text and assess its quality. You will also be able to identify the main points of the text, which in turn allows you to relay information to students. This applies across specialisms – good reading skills will enhance your teaching ability for almost every subject.

Since comprehension skills are important in both of these aspects of teaching, you need to be assessed on it before you become a teacher.

Essentially, the comprehension section tests your ability to do the following:

- Read the text and identify key points;
- Distinguish fact from opinion;
- Understand the content to a degree which allows you to summarise it in your own words;
- Make inferences and deductions based on the information given;
- Identify readership and/or rewrite information for a different target audience;
- Evaluate which points are more important than others;
- Assess contradictions, implied statements and support statements.

All of these skills are important for a teacher, and therefore the comprehension section of the test has questions which will measure your ability. In this chapter, you will learn how to identify specific devices which will be relevant for the comprehension section of the literacy skills test.

While you will learn some helpful methods of answering the comprehension questions, there is no real trick to acing this section of the paper. The best way to practice for it – apart from the sample questions supplied – is to read regularly. Read non-fiction in the form of newspaper/online articles, and bear the above skills in mind. The more you read, the more familiar you will become with how texts are structured and how arguments are formulated.

The next time you read a newspaper article or any other kind of non-fiction piece, keep an eye out for some of the features listed above. Try and spot the key points, separate the fact from opinion and so on. If you're feeling adventurous, you could try to re-write parts of the article in your own words. Practising in this way will help your comprehension skills and assist in preparing you for the test.

In this chapter, we will outline the nine types of question that you may face in the comprehension section. After this, you will be presented with a passage similar to one which you might encounter in the test, as well as some sample questions. Explanations for each kind of question will be given.

When you've finished familiarising yourself with the questions and attempted them for yourself, turn to the end of the chapter to find the answers and explanations for each of the sample questions.

What kind of questions will I be asked?

As previously mentioned, there are nine types of question that can appear in the comprehension section of the literacy skills test. These are:

- Present the main points of a text;
- Match the content of the text (e.g. one or two paragraphs) to a summary;
- Highlight the meanings of words and phrases;

- Sequence information from the text (put it in the right order);
- Complete a list based on the content of the text;
- Attribute statements to elements of the text;
- Choose suitable headings/subheadings;
- Judge statements made about the text;
- Consider readership or target audience.

While there are nine types of question, not all of them will appear in your test. In the actual test, you will only face three kinds of question. However, since you have no way of telling which you'll face, you must prepare for all of them. These categories may seem daunting, but you will become acquainted with them in this chapter.

Lastly, the comprehension section of the paper is worth between ten and twelve marks in total. So, while it might not hold as much value as the punctuation section, the comprehension questions still contain enough marks to separate a successful test from an unsuccessful one. Therefore, give this section of the test as much attention as the others.

Comprehension Tips

When answering the comprehension section of the test, make sure to read the entire text closely. You should read through the entire text before looking at the questions, so that you can understand the overall tone and context of the passage. After reading through it once, take a look at the questions and then re-read the text, bearing the questions in mind.

Comprehension – Sample Questions

The text will be used for all sample questions in this chapter. Make sure to read through the whole passage first before attempting any questions.

The following text is an article from a fictional education journal:

The school have opted to introduce the "20th Century Awareness Project", starting with the "First World War Awareness Programme." The aim these two projects is to strengthen younger students' understanding of the events of the 20th Century.

The school's leadership team believed it was necessary to better teach the history of the 20th Century to all students, particularly the period of 1900-1918. This was due to concerns that younger pupils would not naturally be exposed to the First World War in a sensitive manner, and that depictions of it in popular culture (e.g. film, video-games, television programmes) might not convey the horrors of the war enough, instead choosing to glorify conflict as a whole.

Mrs. Brown, the school's head teacher, claimed that the First World War was "the most important event in recent history" as it shaped the modern world. To an extent, Mrs. Brown's statement is correct. The League of Nations was founded in 1920 mostly as a response to the events of the First World War, which in turn set a precedent for multinational legislative bodies such as the European Union and the United Nations. Additionally, Germany's defeat in the war and subsequent reparation expenses arguably resulted in the rise of the Nazi party and therefore the Second World War, which would shape the world even further.

Mrs. Brown continued, expressing concern that younger pupils might not be learning about the war outside of school. She argued that if we fail to pass on our understanding of such terrible events to younger generations, people in the future won't know the lessons that we've learnt from history.

The school's decision to create a greater focus on the First World War in both history lessons and PSHE (Personal Social Health Education) classes was received well by most teachers as well as a number of students. Teachers have opted to keep the teaching of the First World War interesting by using roleplays and documentaries.

As part of this initiative, the school has decided to devote four assemblies each year to 20th Century history to supplement the focus in lessons. The goal was to provide context to the First World War by discussing events which preceded and followed it. While they were received less favourably than the lessons, these sessions could be more light-hearted and therefore counterbalanced the sombre tone of the First World War lessons.

The final part of the initiative was to promote the teaching of the war and 20th Century history outside of school, with Mrs. Brown urging parents and guardians to visit important historical sites with their children. "By taking our young people to places such as Ypres, we can ensure that they fully understand the cost of war, and make sure that major conflicts like the First and Second world wars never happen again."

Moving forward, the school hopes that these initiatives will do the following:

- Increase the number of students interested in studying History at A-level and university;

- Make students more aware of good and bad depictions of the war in popular culture;

- Make PSHE a more credible lesson in the school;

- Inspire other schools to follow suit and create a stronger focus on 20th Century history.

Presenting the Main Points of a Text

Questions of this kind will ask you to choose from a selection of statements which match the main points of a text. In the test, you will have to pick four statements and drag them into empty boxes.

[   ] Teachers and students approved of the new lesson focus.

[   ] Parents/guardians should make their children aware of the First World War.

[   ] The school has decided to create a larger focus on 20th Century history.

[   ] The assemblies weren't as well-received as the lessons.

[   ] Young students might not be exposed to the history of the war in a sensitive manner.

[   ] The First World War is one of the most important events in recent history.

[   ] The goal of the assemblies was to provide context to the history lessons.

[   ] If we fail to pass our information to future generations, the lessons we've learnt won't carry over either.

[   ] The assemblies were more light-hearted than the lessons.

Matching the Content of the Text to a Summary

For this kind of question, you will be asked to refer to certain paragraphs from the text, and then choose a summary from the selection of answers which matches it best.

Refer to paragraphs 4 and 5. Which of these summaries best suits them?

[   ] Young pupils need to learn about the war outside of school.

[   ] Teachers have opted to use documentaries and roleplays to keep the new classes interesting.

[   ] The head teacher was concerned that students were not learning enough about the First World War outside of school. The new classes' focus on it was received well.

[   ] Parents/Guardians should assist in teaching their children about 20th Century history.

Highlighting the Meaning of Words and Phrases

Questions of this kind will usually highlight part of a sentence from the paragraph, and then ask you to choose from a list of alternative phrases. By doing this, you are showing that you understand the meanings of the words used in the text, since you can substitute them for different phrases.

Re-read the following phrase from paragraph 6 and choose the phrase which is closest to it in meaning.

"... and therefore counterbalanced the sombre tone of the First World War lessons."

☐ ... And therefore reduced the sombre tone...

☐ ... And therefore compensated for the sombre tone...

☐ ... And therefore added to the sombre tone...

☐ ... And therefore had overridden the sombre tone...

Sequencing Information from the Text

This type of question expects you to choose statements which represent the order of information in the passage. This could be a sequence of steps written in the text, or the sequence of information given.

For this question, list the three steps in the school's initiative to increase awareness of 20th Century history. Mark them as "FIRST" "SECOND" and "THIRD".

☐ Create a focus on 20th Century history in all lessons.

☐ Create a focus on the First World War in History and PSHE lessons.

☐ Take students on school trips to important historical sites.

☐ Encourage parents/guardians to teach their children about 20th Century history.

[   ] Promote elements of popular culture which depict the First World War in a positive light.

[   ] Devote assemblies to discussion about 20th Century history.

[   ] Create a focus on 20th Century history in all History classes.

Completing a List based on the Content of the Text

When attempting this type of question, you will need to choose statements which complete a list of bullet points found in the passage. For this question, the third point has been filled in for you.

•

•

•   Make PSHE a more credible lesson in the school.

•

[   ] Urge parents to get involved in the teaching of their children.

[   ] Decrease focus on the Middle Ages in History lessons.

[   ] Increase awareness for different kinds of depiction about the war.

[   ] Make assemblies more interesting.

[   ] Be an example to other schools.

[   ] Encourage more students to study history.

[   ] Reduce troublemakers in lessons.

Attributing Statements to Elements of the Text

This type of question involves elements of the text (often categories) which must be matched with a selection of statements. For this example, write the number in the box. For the actual test, you will need to drag an abbreviation for the element into the box next to the statement.

Read the following statements and decide which refer to:

1. The League of Nations
2. The 20th Century Awareness Project
3. The First World War Awareness Programme
4. PSHE

[____] A project with the aim of changing the school's overall focus regarding history.

[____] Personal Social Health Education.

[____] A project devoted to changing the focus of history and PSHE lessons.

[____] A multinational body formed after the First World War.

Choosing Suitable Headings and Subheadings

For this kind of question, you will be expected to choose a heading or subheading from a selection. This could be an overall heading for the entire piece, or possibly a subheading for a specific paragraph or portion of the text. Try to choose a heading/subheading which suits the text both in terms of tone and content.

Choose the most suitable heading for the entire text:

[____] War is Hell.

[____] Head teacher urges parents to teach their children about the war.

[____] School's focus on First World War is met with good reception.

[____] Remembering the Fallen.

Choose the most suitable subheading for paragraph 3:

[____] Why the First World War matters.

[____] Head teacher reminds us of the importance of the First World War.

[____] How the Nazi's rose to power.

[____] A brief history of the 20th Century.

Judging Statements about the Text

This type of question will ask you to evaluate a selection of statements made about the text. You must decide if these statements are supported by the text, implicitly supported (implied), unsupported by the text, implicitly contradicted or explicitly contradicted.

Use the following abbreviations to evaluate the statements:

S   – is supported by the text.

I   – is implied by the text.

NE – is unsupported by the text (no evidence for it).

IC – is implicitly contradicted by the text.

EC – is explicitly contradicted by the text.

| | The League of Nations was founded in 1920.

| | The overall initiative was a success.

| | The more sombre tone of the First World War inspired teachers to make light-hearted activities for students, such as roleplays.

| | The assemblies were well received.

| | Parents/guardians were frequently assisting in their child's education regarding 20th Century history.

Considering Readership and Target Audience

Questions following this format will expect you to identify the most suitable audience for the text. You will also need to highlight the least suitable audience for the text.

Use the following notation to show which audience is most suitable and which audience is least suitable:

MS – Most suitable.

LS – Least suitable.

- [ ] Government officials.
- [ ] Other head teachers/leadership teams in nearby schools.
- [ ] Parents/guardians of students in the school.
- [ ] Trainee teachers.

Comprehension – Answers and Explanations

In this section you will find answers for the comprehension sample questions. Explanations have been included for each question, so that you can understand the reasoning used.

Presenting the Main Points of a Text

The main points of the text are as follows:

1. Parents/guardians should make their children aware of the First World War.

The reasoning for this is that the entire final paragraph is devoted to this point. It is also accompanied by one of the few quotes in the text, signifying its importance further. More importantly, the paragraph denotes this point as the final part of the initiative, which further suggests that it is one of the main points of the text.

2. The school has decided to create a larger focus on 20th Century history.

This is considered a main point because it is the aim of one of the main projects listed at the start of the text. The subject of the entire text revolves around this point.

3. Young students might not be exposed to the history of the war in a sensitive manner.

This is the focus of paragraph 4, and is one of the main points because it is the motivation for both of the projects introduced in the first paragraph. Since the entire text is focused on these two projects, the reason for introducing them is an important point for the texts.

4. The First World War is one of the most important events in recent history.

This is a main point because it is the subject of a major paragraph (paragraph 3) and includes a quote. It is also part of the head teacher's motivation for introducing the programme.

Other Points

When looking for the main points of a text, keep an eye out for the main initiatives, programmes or strategies referenced. Also make sure that your choices include points which are in the passage – it is possible that some of the choices are not actually explicit in the text.

Be sure to re-read each paragraph, since main points tend to be the focus of at least one paragraph. It would be unusual for someone to write a text with a main point which only had one sentence devoted to it.

Once you've chosen what you believe to be the main points of the text, read them back to yourself and consider if they cover the majority of the text's material. If it helps, it might be worth imagining that you had to summarise this text to someone over the telephone. Would your choices include the essential things people need to know about the text?

In some cases, it may seem as though most (or perhaps even all) of the choices given could be main points. In this scenario, choose the points which seem to be the most important.

Matching the Content of the Text to a Summary

The most suitable summary for paragraphs 4 and 5 is:

3. The head teacher was concerned that students were not learning enough about the First World War outside of school. The new classes' focus on it were received well.

This summary is most suitable since it encompasses the main points of the two paragraphs. The focus of paragraph 4 is on the head teacher's concern about students' understanding of the First World War, while paragraph 5 covers the success of these classes. Therefore, this summary is quite adequate.

The other summaries are less adequate, because they either a) don't provide a summary of the paragraphs in question, or b) don't focus on the main points of the two paragraphs.

The first and last choices focus on the main points of other paragraphs. While they might suit those paragraphs, they do not provide a summary of paragraphs 4 and 5.

In comparison, the second choice contains content from paragraph 5, but not paragraph 4. Therefore, it is not an adequate summary. Even if it did include content from paragraph 4, it might still be considered insufficient since it does not focus on the key point of paragraph 5: that the new lessons were well-received.

Other Points

When trying to find a suitable summary, make sure it encompasses the key points of all the paragraphs you have been asked to find a summary for. The aim of a summary is to compile the most important points as briefly as possible. Shorter summaries may be preferable, but only if they cover everything they need to.

Highlighting the Meaning of Words and Phrases

The closest substitute for the given phrase is:

2. ... And therefore compensated for the sombre tone...

This choice is most suitable because 'compensated' is a synonym for 'counter balanced.'

The other choices were unsuitable because they do not mean the same thing. The first choice uses the word 'reduced,' which suggests that the sombre tone of the First World War lessons was lessened by the light-hearted assemblies. However, this is not the case: these assemblies acted as a counterbalance. While they did not add to the sombre tone of the First World War (as the third choice suggests), they did not actively work against it either. Instead, these assemblies acted as some relief from the more serious tone of the lessons.

Likewise, the fourth choice uses the word 'overridden,' which implies that these assemblies outweighed the tone of the lessons. Again, this is not what the original phrase is saying. Rather than dominating the tone of the lessons, the assemblies acted as a counterbalance, which suggests that they are approximately equal. Therefore, the fourth choice is also unsuitable.

Other Points

This kind of question can be tricky, since it requires an understanding of what specific words mean. However, it's almost impossible to predict which words you need to know. If you are unsure of what the word means, look for the context in the sentence – sometimes you can figure out what the word means by how it's used.

In addition, be sure to re-read the paragraph the phrase belongs to, or even the wider text, since they might give a clue of what the word means. For example, if the phrase in the question used the word 'dismal' to describe something, and you weren't sure what the word meant, another part of the text may have another description of the same thing, which in turn might provide a hint.

Sequencing Information from the Text

The correct choices in order are:

2. Create a focus on the First World War in all History and PSHE lessons. FIRST.

6. Devote assemblies to discussion about 20th Century history. SECOND.

4. Encourage parents/guardians to teach their children about 20th Century history. THIRD.

The other points are incorrect since they are not supported by the text (1, 3), or are not made explicit by it (5, 7). Generally speaking, the sequencing of information questions will require you to find points which are explicitly referred to, rather than have to make inferences about the information being sequenced.

Other Points

For this question, look for clues in the text which reveal the steps in the process. Generally speaking, the order of the steps will flow logically through the text – it's unlikely that the third step in the process will be listed first. Moreover, the text may denote the steps as "firstly…", "secondly…" and so on.

Also make sure that your choices only include steps which are found in the text. It's possible that some of the choices will not be points in the text, and therefore they cannot be suitable answers for this question.

Completing a List based on the Content of the Text

To finish the list, you must choose the following:

6. *Encourage more students to study History.*

3. *Increase awareness for different kinds of depiction about the war.*

5. *Be an example to other schools.*

The answers above are worded slightly differently to how they appear in the main text. This could be the case in the test, and therefore you must be able to match the paraphrased answers with the bullet points in the text. Therefore, make sure you re-read the list of bullet points in order to identify the correct phrasings.

The other choices were incorrect because they didn't include information from the list. You should only choose answers which contain content from the list.

Other Points

For this kind of question, you only need to focus on the list featured in the text – you can ignore the other content for the time being. However, make sure you have read the entire text at least once before attempting this question, since it can provide some context for the list, making it easier to spot the correct paraphrased answers.

Attributing Statements to Elements of the Text

The correct answers are as follows:

The League of Nations	A multinational body formed after the First World War.
The 20th Century Awareness Project	A project with the aim of changing the school's overall focus regarding history.
The First World War Awareness Programme	A project devoted to changing the focus of History and PSHE lessons.
PSHE	Personal Social Health Education.

Other Points

For this kind of question, read the entire text in order to find statements which match the elements given. These elements are usually categories of some kind such as groups of people (e.g. qualified teachers, trainee teachers) or projects or programmes such as those given in the sample question.

Choosing Suitable Headings and Subheadings

The most suitable heading for the entire test is:

3. School's focus on First World War is met with good reception.

This heading is the most suitable since it adequately explains the main point of the text (that the school has placed more emphasis on the First World War) and the major result of it (it is well-received). Moreover, since the text is from a fictional teaching journal, it needs a shorter title to remain interesting. Therefore, option 2 is unsuitable.

The first and fourth options are also unsuitable since they are too dramatic and do not match the message of the text. Option 1 bears little relevance to the text, and while option 4 is slightly more relevant, it doesn't outline the content of the text.

The most suitable subheading for paragraph 3 is:

1. Why the First World War matters.

Again, this subheading is most suitable since it is shorter than option 2, and adequately introduces the main point of the paragraph. The third option does not represent the message of the paragraph, since it isn't focused on the Nazi party's rise to power, and option 4 is far too vague.

Other Points

For questions of this kind, keep an eye out for the target audience. The text may be introduced as a journal article, a government document, or possibly even a school newsletter. The kind of text will contribute to what kind of heading or subheading is most suitable. Government documents may use more technical jargon, while newsletters will opt for a shorter title with simpler words to be more effective.

Regardless of the text's source, relevant titles are always preferable to overdramatic, irrelevant ones.

Judging Statements about the Text

The correct answers for this sample question are:

The League of Nations was founded in 1920. – S

The overall initiative was a success. – NE

The more sombre tone of the First World War inspired teachers to make light-hearted activities for students, such as roleplays. – I

The assemblies were well received. – EC

Parents/guardians were frequently assisting in their child's education regarding 20th Century history. - IC

- *"The League of Nations was founded in 1920."* This is supported by the text since it is explicit in paragraph 3.

- *"The overall initiative was a success."* This is not supported or contradicted by the text. We know from the text that the classes were well-received and the assemblies were poorly received, but we cannot tell if the goals of the initiative listed at the end of the text were met. Therefore, there is no evidence in the text that supports this statement.

- *"The more sombre tone of the First World War inspired teachers to make light-hearted activities for students, such as roleplays."* While not made explicit in the text, we can make this inference since it is mentioned that the First World War lessons had a sombre tone in paragraph 6. We also know that teachers introduced roleplays from paragraph 5, and therefore we can infer that these were used to keep the classes light-hearted in tone.

- *"The assemblies were well received."* This is explicitly contradicted by the text, as we can see from paragraph 6.

- *"Parents/guardians were frequently assisting in their child's education regarding 20th Century history."* This is implicitly contradicted by the text, since the head teacher is urging parents/guardians to help in making their children more aware of 20th Century events.

Other Points

This kind of question may be one of the most demanding of the whole section, since it requires you to read the entire text very closely. More importantly, you need to be clear on what the different attributes (implied, explicitly contradicted etc.) mean.

Supported by the text:

This simply means that the text provides explicit evidence for the statement. If the text says that the League of Nations was founded in 1920, and one of the statements says the same thing, then the statement is supported by the text.

Implied by the text:

This means that the text gives implicit evidence for the statement. Unlike statements supported by the text, this means that the statement is supported but it isn't entirely clear. For this, you may need to "read between the lines" in order to figure out what statements the text implicitly supports.

For example, if the text stated that older students were more receptive to the First World War lessons than younger students, the implication would be that the younger students didn't particularly enjoy the lessons.

Unsupported by the text (no evidence):

This means that the text offers no evidence to support the statement, and also offers no evidence to contradict or refute the statement. Simply put, there is no way to confirm whether the statement is true or false based purely on the information in the text.

Explicitly contradicted by the text:

The statement is directly refuted by information in the text. If the text says that the assemblies were poorly received, and the statement says that the assemblies were well-received, then there is a contradiction. Since this contradiction is clear or explicit, then the statement is explicitly contradicted by the test.

It may help to think of this as the opposite of "supported by the text," which means that the statement is clearly supported by the information in the text. In this case, the information in the text clearly opposes the statement.

Implicitly contradicted by the text:

Similar to the explicit contradiction, this means that the statement is contradicted by the text, although it might not be clear. For example, if the text shows the head teacher urging parents to assist in making their children more aware of 20th Century history, then the implication is that parents are currently not doing so. So, if the statement claims that parents are helping, then there is an implicit contradiction.

In a sense, this is the opposite of "implied by the text," but in this case the text implicitly opposes the statement rather than implicitly supports it.

Considering Readership and Target Audience

The most and least suitable target audiences are:

MS – Other head teachers/leadership teams in nearby schools.

LS – Trainee teachers.

Since the text is an article from an education journal, it is most suitable for teachers who have an interest in the wider teaching community. Moreover, since the school is trying to set an example for other schools (as mentioned in the list), it makes most sense for other leadership teams to be the target readership for the article.

Trainee teachers are the least suitable since, while the article may be interesting for them to read, it won't have as much of an impact on them as parents and guardians in the school community who want to know about the current events of the school. Likewise, government officials are a slightly more suitable target audience, since the programme could be brought into the national curriculum if successful.

Other Points

Target audience can be determined by a number of factors. Firstly, large amounts of jargon might suggest that the audience is for specialists such as government officials. Simpler vocabulary might suggest a target audience of younger or less specialised people, such as parents or perhaps trainee teachers.

Secondly, the introduction of the text may give a hint as to what the intended readership is. The text used in this section is from a fictional education journal, which suggests that the target audience is intended to be teachers rather than parents. If the source came from a school newsletter, then it's likely written with parents in mind.

Finally, make note of the content of the text overall when determining target audience. Who is the content relevant to? The text would not be useful for students within the school, since they are already experiencing the new programmes and therefore do not need an article to tell them about it.

Conclusion

The comprehension section may be the most demanding part of the entire literacy skills test. However, if you have followed the advice in this section, attempted the sample questions and followed the advice in the answers section, you should be in a good position for the test.

Keep reading for a glossary, as well as your mock QTS literacy skills test!

THE QTS LITERACY SKILLS TEST
MOCK TEST

Introduction

Now that you are familiar with the material of the QTS literacy skills test as well as the type of questions you might face, it's time to attempt the mock test. While the real test is computerised, as much as possible has been done to make sure that this test represents it as best as possible. However, bear the following in mind before taking the mock test:

- In the real test, you will usually have to drag and drop your answers into spaces in the text. In this version, you will have to write your answers in the book or on your notes;

- Both audio and non-audio versions of the spelling section have been provided to accommodate your own needs. If you wish to take the audio version of the spelling section, use the following link to find the audio files you will need to listen to: http://www.qtsspellingtest.co.uk/

- Do not attempt both the audio and non-audio versions of the spelling section, since you will only have to do one or the other in the real test;

- You have 45 minutes to complete the test. Find a clock or a watch to time yourself. If possible, get a stopwatch to time yourself for each section. By doing this, you will have an idea of how long each section takes you and where you need to improve;

- In the real test, you may be entitled to extra time depending on your circumstances. If you have a disability or some other form of sensory impairment which may hinder your ability to do the test, you may be entitled to 25% additional time. If this applies to you, 57 minutes are available to complete the test;

- If you have a disability which severely impacts your ability to do the test, you may be entitled to an extra 50% additional time. If this applies to you, 68 minutes are available to complete the test. Be aware that this extra 50% is only given under rare circumstances.

Section 1 – Spelling (Non-Audio Version)

There are ten marks available for this section. Once you have finished this section, you may not return to it.

1. Many were _ _ _ _ _ _ _ _ _ _ _ _ _ _ _ _ _ by the news.

- Dissappointed
- Disappointed
- Disapointed
- Disepointed

2. The best students had been invited to a special awards
_ _ _ _ _ _ _ _ _ _ _ _ _ _ _ _ _ _ _.

- Ceremony
- Seramony
- Seremony
- Sayramony

3. The good results came as a _ _ _ _ _ _ _ _ _ _ _ _ _ _ _ _ _ to both staff and students.

- Suprise
- Surpreyes
- Surprise
- Serprise

4. The teaching in the English department had been _ _ _ _ _ _ _ _ _ _ _ _ _ _ _ _ _ _
   that term.

   • Exceptional
   • Acceptional
   • Excepsional
   • Exeptional

5. There was a distinct lack of _ _ _ _ _ _ _ _ _ _ _ _ _ _ _ _ _ amongst the students.

   • Rispect
   • Raspect
   • Respect
   • Ruspect

6. Most of the changes to the curriculum were _ _ _ _ _ _ _ _ _ _ _ _ _ _ _ _ _ _.

   • Unessessary
   • Unecessary
   • Unnessesary
   • Unnecessary

7. Very few people had _ _ _ _ _ _ _ _ _ _ _ _ _ _ _ for the role.

   • Applied
   • Appleyed
   • Aplied
   • Applyed

8. There was a marked _ _ _ _ _ _ _ _ _ _ _ _ _ _ _ _ _ in the quality of the canteen food.

- Improovement
- Improvement
- Improvment
- Improovment

9. Her teaching methods were _ _ _ _ _ _ _ _ _ _ _ _ _ _ _ _ _ _.

- Unnconventional
- Unconventional
- Unconvensional
- Uncunvensional

10. The new uniform rules had a negative impact on some of the more
_ _ _ _ _ _ _ _ _ _ _ _ _ _ _ _ _ students.

- Ecksentric
- Ecsentric
- Eccentric
- Eczendric

Section 1 – Spelling (Audio Version)

There are ten marks available for this section. Once you have finished this section, you may not return to it.

Use your headphones to listen to the missing words, and then write them how you believe them to be spelled.

1. Many were _ _ _ _ _ _ _ _ _ _ _ _ _ _ _ _ _ _ by the news.

2. The best students had been invited to a special awards
_ _ _ _ _ _ _ _ _ _ _ _ _ _ _ _ _ _.

3. The good results came as a _ _ _ _ _ _ _ _ _ _ _ _ _ _ _ _ to both staff and
students.

4. The teaching in the English department had been _ _ _ _ _ _ _ _ _ _ _ _ _ _ _ _ _ _
that term.

5. There was a distinct lack of _ _ _ _ _ _ _ _ _ _ _ _ _ _ _ _ _ amongst the students.

6. Most of the changes to the curriculum were _ _ _ _ _ _ _ _ _ _ _ _ _ _ _ _ _ _.

7. Very few people had _ _ _ _ _ _ _ _ _ _ _ _ _ _ _ _ _ for the role.

8. There was a marked _ _ _ _ _ _ _ _ _ _ _ _ _ _ _ _ _ in the quality of the canteen
food.

9. Her teaching methods were _ _ _ _ _ _ _ _ _ _ _ _ _ _ _ _ _ _.

10. The new uniform rules had a negative impact on some of the more
_ _ _ _ _ _ _ _ _ _ _ _ _ _ _ _ _ students.

Section 2 – Punctuation

There are fifteen marks available for this section.

The following passage is lacking fifteen pieces of punctuation. Add punctuation to the text where you feel it is necessary. If you want to show that a capital letter is needed, circle the letter which should be capitalised and then write 'cap' or 'capital' in the margin. If a new paragraph is necessary, put two forward slashes (//) after the end of the paragraph and then write 'NP' in the margin.

So far twelve students had been given detention time for being excessively late for lessons in particular henry had been given after-school detentions for 2 weeks for showing up late to PSHE lessons, which he had described as a waste of time The new statistics for lesson performance were also rather worrying they showed that students were not paying attention at all in PSHE the school will have to reconsider their strategy in the way they teach their students about societal issues the head teacher mrs Brown was preparing a meeting to address the problem

Section 3 – Grammar

There are ten marks available for this section.

The following passages have parts missing. For each blank line, choose the answer which is the most suitable from a grammatical perspective.

Exercise A

1. *Firstly, it has been made clear that...*

_____

_____

A. *rules regarding the new school uniform have not been followed by students.*

B. *rules regarding the new school uniform has not been follow by students.*

C. *rules regarding the new school uniform has not been followed by students.*

D. *rules regarding the new school uniform have not been follow by students.*

2. *Measures will be taken to...*

_____

_____

A. *ensure that all pupils are wearing their ties at the correct length and are not wearing brown shoes because they are no longer allowed.*

B. *insure that all pupils are wearing their ties at the correct length and are not wearing brown shoes because they are no longer allowed.*

C. *ensure that pupils are wearing their ties at the correct length and are not wearing brown shoes because only black shoes are allowed.*

D. *insure that pupils are wearing their ties at the correct length and are not wearing brown shoes because only black shoes are allowed.*

3. *There are plenty of students who are following these new rules to the letter...*

_____

_____

A. *Moreover, there are still too many who are not paying attention to these new rules.*

B. *However, there are still too many who are not paying attention to these new rules.*

C. *Consequently, there are still too many who are not paying attention to these new rules.*

D. *In addition, there are still too many who are not paying attention to these new rules.*

4. *Uniform standards...*

_____

_____

A. *are taken very seriously by the school since they shows that students are ready to learn.*

B. *are taken very seriously by the school since it shows that students are ready to learn.*

C. *is taken very seriously by the school since it shows that students are ready to learn.*

D. *are taken very seriously by the school since they show that students are ready to learn.*

Exercise B

1.   *The role of this new government programme is to...*

_____

_____

A. *change the grade boundaries for GCSE results to represent the standards of the population best than the current system.*

B. *change the grade boundaries for GCSE results to represent the standards of the population better than the current system.*

C. *change the grade boundary for GCSE results to represent the standards of the population better than the current system.*

D. *change the grade boundary for GCSE results to represent the standards of the population best than the current system.*

2.   *By making it easier to attain an E to C grade, but harder to achieve between a B and an A,...*

_____

_____

A. *there would be less students failing their GCSEs and this would mean that more young people could move into schemes of employment such as apprenticeships.*

B. *there would be fewer students failing their GCSEs and this would mean that more young people could move into schemes of employment such as apprenticeships.*

C. *there would be less students failing their GCSEs. This would mean that more young people could move into schemes of employment such as apprenticeships.*

D. *there would be fewer students failing their GCSEs. This would mean that more young people could move into schemes of employment such as apprenticeships.*

3. *In addition, hopefully more students would accept the new challenge and strive for higher grades...*

A. *Although there were more young people staying on school. Too few were achieving higher grades and going to top universities.*

B. *Although there were more young people staying on school, too few were achieving higher grades and going to top universities.*

C. *Although there were more young people staying in school, too few were achieving higher grades and going to top universities.*

D. *Although there were more young people staying in school. Too few were achieving higher grades and going to top universities.*

Exercise C

1. *If we change the History curriculum to include more 20th Century history,...*

_____

_____

A. *there is the added bonus that students will learn about the events of the First and Second World Wars. The older students should have learned about them by now.*

B. *there is the bonus that students will learn about the events of the First and Second World Wars. The older students should have learned about it by now.*

C. *there is the added bonus that students will learn about the events of the First and Second World Wars. The older students should of learned about them by now.*

D. *there is the bonus that students will learn about the events of the First and Second World Wars. The older students should have learned about them by now.*

2. *By this point, many of the students and teachers are bored of the Tudors...*

_____

_____

A. *By moving onto something far more recent and relevant, they might be inclined to pay more attention. This would also prevent them from going crazy in the afternoon lessons.*

B. *By moving onto something far more recent and relevant, the students might be inclined to pay more attention. This would also prevent them from being uncontrollable in the afternoon lessons.*

C. *By moving onto something far more recent and relevant, the students might be inclined to pay more attention. This would also prevent from going crazy in the afternoon lessons.*

D. *By moving onto something far more recent and relevant, they might be inclined to pay more attention. This would also prevent them from being uncontrollable in the afternoon lessons.*

3. *Students, parents and governors have shown approval at this new plan....*

_____

_____

A. *However, the leadership team will be meeting about changing the curriculum today.*

B. *Therefore, the leadership team will be meeting today about changing the curriculum.*

C. *In spite of this, the leadership team will be meeting today about changing the curriculum.*

D. *Furthermore, the leadership team will be meeting about changing the curriculum today.*

Section 4 - Comprehension

There are ten marks available for this section of the test.

The following text is part of a fictional report, written by a teacher, making a case against the use of isolation in the school which the teacher works at. Read the text carefully, and then answer the questions provided.

Currently, the only way that the school placates some of the more troublesome students is by placing them in isolation. However, as many of the teachers have pointed out, isolation is far from an ideal solution. The reasons for this include:

- *Isolation is considered inhumane, with some even comparing it to solitary confinement;*

- *By isolating certain students, they are not acquiring the social skills needed to co-operate in a classroom and in wider society;*

- *As a result of the above point, many students end up returning to isolation frequently over the course of a term;*

- *Isolation prevents the individual student from learning. A student falls behind because they are not in the classroom, and therefore they struggle to engage with the material. As a result, students are more likely to misbehave;*

- *When a student returns to a class after isolation, a surge in disruption is usually felt as other students stop working to ask questions.*

With all of the above in mind, the benefits of isolation do not appear particularly advantageous. For example, one of the supposed positives of isolating troublesome students is that removing them allows the rest of the class to continue with their work. Admittedly, this can be incredibly useful in the short term, as the more difficult students have a tendency to disrupt entire classes.

However, this is merely a short-term solution. It is certainly helpful while the student is in isolation, but the problems highlighted above demonstrate that the short-term solution is matched with long-term implications. For this reason, we need an alternative method for dealing with troublesome students.

Exercise A

From the options given below, complete the bulleted list. Leave a tick next to each option which you believe to be correct. The first bullet point has been completed for you.

- A number of people consider isolation to be inhumane.
-
-
-
-

☐ Isolation results in students causing trouble on the school playground.

☐ Students returning from isolation tend to disrupt classes by being asked questions.

☐ Isolation makes it difficult for a student to re-integrate with a class and work once they return to the classroom.

☐ Isolation helps keep classes calm as troublemakers are removed from the room.

☐ Some students will visit isolation frequently.

☐ Isolation stops students from socialising in a positive way.

Exercise B

Read the following statements. For each statement, decide whether it is supported by the text (S), implied by the text (I) or if there is no evidence for it in the text (NE).

☐ Isolation results in students becoming more violent.

☐ Isolating students makes it more difficult for them to function in society.

☐ The long-term disadvantages of isolation outweigh the advantages.

☐ The school currently only has one method of dealing with troublesome students.

Exercise C

From this list of target audiences, choose the one which is most suitable (MS) and the one which is least suitable (LS).

	Trainee teachers
	Students at the school
	The head teacher/leadership team
	Parents of students at the school

END OF QUESTIONS

THE QTS
LITERACY
SKILLS TEST
MOCK TEST
ANSWERS AND
EXPLANATIONS

Introduction

Once you've attempted the mock test, compare your responses with the correct answers in this answers section. If you find that you have answered a significant number of questions incorrectly, do not panic. Return to the material that has been outlined in earlier chapters, understand why your answer is incorrect, and then attempt the questions again. Where applicable, explanations for the correct answers have been given in this section.

Section 1 – Spelling

1. Many were **disappointed** by the news.

2. The best students had been invited to a special awards **ceremony**.

3. The good results came as a **surprise** to both staff and students.

4. The teaching in the English department had been **exceptional** that term.

5. There was a distinct lack of **respect** amongst the students.

6. Most of the changes to the curriculum were **unnecessary**.

7. Very few people had **applied** for the role.

8. There was a marked **improvement** in the quality of the canteen food.

9. Her teaching methods were **unconventional**.

10. The new uniform rules had a negative impact on some of the more **eccentric** students.

Section 2 – Punctuation

So far, twelve students had been given detention time for being excessively late for lessons. In particular, Henry had been given after-school detentions for 2 weeks for showing up late to PSHE lessons, which he had described as a 'waste of time'.

(New Paragraph)

The new statistics for lesson performance were also rather worrying: they showed that students were not paying attention at all in PSHE. The school will have to reconsider their strategy in the way they teach their students about societal issues; the head teacher Mrs Brown was preparing a meeting to address the problem.

Section 3 – Grammar

Exercise A

1. *Firstly, it has been made clear that...*

A. *rules regarding the new school uniform have not been followed by students.*

B. *rules regarding the new school uniform has not been follow by students.*

C. *rules regarding the new school uniform has not been followed by students.*

D. *rules regarding the new school uniform have not been follow by students.*

The correct answer to this question is A. This is because the subject and verb are in agreement. Since 'rules' is plural, 'have' is correct while 'has' is incorrect. This means that answers B and C are unsatisfactory.

Additionally, question A is consistent with the introductory line's use of tense. The introductory line *('Firstly, it has been made clear that')* uses the past tense, and therefore the past tense verb for 'follow' should be used ('followed'). Therefore, answer D is also unsuitable.

2. *Measures will be taken to...*

A. *ensure that all pupils are wearing their ties at the correct length and are not wearing brown shoes because they are no longer allowed.*

B. *insure that all pupils are wearing their ties at the correct length and are not wearing brown shoes because they are no longer allowed.*

C. *ensure that pupils are wearing their ties at the correct length and are not wearing brown shoes because only black shoes are allowed.*

D. *insure that pupils are wearing their ties at the correct length and are not wearing brown shoes because only black shoes are allowed.*

For this question, the correct answer is C. This is for two reasons. Firstly, its use of 'ensure' is correct, whilst the use of 'insure' in answers B and D is incorrect. This is an example of two commonly confused words. To ensure something is to make sure that something does or does not happen. In comparison, to insure something is protect it with insurance. Therefore, options B and D are not suitable.

Furthermore, answers A and B use ambiguous pronouns. The use of 'they' could be referring to incorrect tie length or brown shoes, which could cause confusion. Answer C rewords the sentence slightly to prevent this ambiguity. Therefore, answer C is the most suitable for this sentence.

3. *There are plenty of students who are following these new rules to the letter...*

A. *Moreover, there are still too many who are not paying attention to these new rules.*

B. **However, there are still too many who are not paying attention to these new rules.**

C. *Consequently, there are still too many who are not paying attention to these new rules.*

D. *In addition, there are still too many who are not paying attention to these new rules.*

The correct answer for this question is B. This is because it makes correct use of cohesive devices, and is therefore most cohesive with the introductory sentence. The subject matter of the answer sentence does not reinforce the information in the introductory sentence, and therefore 'moreover' and 'in addition' given in answers A and D respectively are incorrect. The information in answer sentence is not a result of the information in the introductory sentence, and therefore 'consequently' is also incorrect.

4. *Uniform standards...*

A. *are taken very seriously by the school since they shows that students are ready to learn.*

B. *are taken very seriously by the school since it shows that students are ready to learn.*

C. *is taken very seriously by the school since it shows that students are ready to learn.*

D. *are taken very seriously by the school since they show that students are ready to learn.*

The correct answer for this question is D. This is because there is an agreement between the verb ('are') and the subject ('uniform standards'). Answer C uses the incorrect verb 'is'.

Additionally, answer D is preferable over B because the correct pronoun is used – 'they'. Since the subject ('uniform standards') is a plural, 'it' is an incorrect pronoun because it addresses a singular.

Finally, answer A is incorrect because there is a disagreement between the form of the verb and the subject. Since the subject is a plural, 'show' should be used rather than 'shows'.

Exercise B

1. *The role of this new government programme is to...*

A. *change the grade boundaries for GCSE results to represent the standards of the population best than the current system.*

B. change the grade boundaries for GCSE results to represent the standards of the population better than the current system.

C. *change the grade boundary for GCSE results to represent the standards of the population better than the current system.*

D. *change the grade boundary for GCSE results to represent the standards of the population best than the current system.*

The correct answer for this question is B. The reason for this is that B makes correct use of comparatives. Answers A and D use the term 'best' (a superlative) instead of 'better' (a comparative). Since the sentence is making a comparison between two entities (the new GCSE grade boundaries and the 'current system'), a comparative is grammatically correct.

In addition, answer C does not pluralise the word 'boundary'. This needs to be pluralised because the boundaries are a property of the GCSE results, which are a plural.

2. *By making it easier to attain an E to C grade, but harder to achieve between a B and an A,...*

A. *there would be less students failing their GCSEs and this would mean that more young people could move into schemes of employment such as apprenticeships.*

B. *there would be fewer students failing their GCSEs and this would mean that more young people could move into schemes of employment such as apprenticeships.*

C. *there would be less students failing their GCSEs. This would mean that more young people could move into schemes of employment such as apprenticeships.*

> **D. *there would be fewer students failing their GCSEs. This would mean that more young people could move into schemes of employment such as apprenticeships.***

For this question, the correct response is D. This is because it pays attention to sentence boundaries and doesn't confuse two words. Answers A and B feature too many clauses in their sentences; there should be a full stop after 'GCSEs'.

This leaves options C and D. Option C misuses the word 'less' when 'fewer' is preferable. This is because, generally speaking, the word 'less' is used when referring to something which is uncountable or a singular such as water, blood or space. In contrast, 'fewer' is used when referring to something which is a plural, such as 'students'. Therefore, D is preferable over C.

> **3.** *In addition, hopefully more students would accept the new challenge and strive for higher grades...*
>
> A. *Although there were more young people staying on school. Too few were achieving higher grades and going to top universities.*
>
> B. *Although there were more young people staying on school, too few were achieving higher grades and going to top universities.*
>
> **C. *Although there were more young people staying in school, too few were achieving higher grades and going to top universities.***
>
> D. *Although there were more young people staying in school. Too few were achieving higher grades and going to top universities.*

C is the correct answer for the following reasons. Firstly, it does not contain a sentence fragment: both A and D feature a full stop after the word 'school', turning the sentence into a fragment. This is a fragment because the word 'although' at the start of the sentence implies that there is a second clause, but there is no second clause in the sentence. Therefore, a comma is preferable.

Moreover, answers A and B use the incorrect preposition. Typically, people stay 'in' school rather than 'on' school. Therefore, A and B are also incorrect.

Exercise C

1. If we change the history curriculum to include more 20th Century history,...

A. *there is the added bonus that students will learn about the events of the First and Second World Wars. The older students should have learned about them by now.*

B. *there is the bonus that students will learn about the events of the First and Second World Wars. The older students should have learned about it by now.*

C. *there is the added bonus that students will learn about the events of the First and Second World Wars. The older students should of learned about them by now.*

D. *there is the bonus that students will learn about the events of the First and Second World Wars. The older students should have learned about them by now.*

D is the correct answer for the following reasons. Firstly, unlike answers A and C, D does not contain the tautology 'added bonus'. All bonuses are additional, and so the word 'added' is redundant. Answer C uses the phrase 'should of' instead of 'should have', which is also incorrect. Finally, answer B makes an incorrect use of pronouns. Since 'the First and Second World Wars' are plural, 'the older students should have learned about them', not 'the older students should have learned about it'.

2. By this point, many of the students and teachers are bored of the Tudors.

A. *By moving onto something far more recent and relevant, they might be inclined to pay more attention. This would also prevent them from going crazy in the afternoon lessons.*

B. *By moving onto something far more recent and relevant, the students might be inclined to pay more attention. This would also prevent them from being uncontrollable in the afternoon lessons.*

C. *By moving onto something far more recent and relevant, the students might be inclined to pay more attention. This would also prevent from going crazy in the afternoon lessons.*

D. *By moving onto something far more recent and relevant, they might be inclined to pay more attention. This would also prevent them from being uncontrollable in the afternoon lessons.*

For this question, answer B is correct. This is because it does not feature ambiguous pronouns. Answers A and D use the phrase 'they', which could refer to the students, teachers or even the Tudors. Clearly, this pronoun is supposed to refer to the students, but this isn't made evident in the sentence.

In addition, answers A and C are inconsistent in tone, since they use the phrase 'going crazy' which appears inappropriate. Answer B uses the phrase 'being uncontrollable' which better describes the behaviour of the students.

3. *Students, parents and governors have shown approval at this new plan.*

A. *However, the leadership team will be meeting about changing the curriculum today.*

B. *Therefore, the leadership team will be meeting today about changing the curriculum.*

C. *In spite of this, the leadership team will be meeting today about changing the curriculum.*

D. *Furthermore, the leadership team will be meeting about changing the curriculum today.*

The correct answer to this question is B. This is the case for two reasons. Firstly, answers A and C use cohesive devices which are inconsistent with the introductory sentence. The leadership team's meeting isn't taking place in spite of or contrary to the approval or students, parents and governors. In fact, it is likely that the meeting is occurring as a result of the approval, so 'therefore' is the most fitting cohesive device.

Furthermore, answer B avoids attachment problems. Answers A and D are ambiguous. On the one hand, they could be meeting today about changing the curriculum. However, they could also be meeting about changing the curriculum today (in other words, today will be the day that the curriculum changes). This ambiguity is resolved by answer B, which clarifies that the meeting is being held today.

Section 4 - Comprehension

Exercise A

To complete the list, you must have chosen the following:

☐ Students returning from isolation tend to disrupt classes by being asked questions.

☐ Isolation makes it difficult for a student to re-integrate with a class and work once they return to the classroom.

☐ Some students will visit isolation frequently.

☐ Isolation stops students from socialising in a positive way.

Exercise B

The following statements have no evidence to support them (NE), are implied by the text (I) or are supported by the text (S):

☐ Isolation results in students becoming more violent. – NE

☐ Isolating students makes it more difficult for them to function in society. – I

☐ The long-term disadvantages of isolation outweigh the advantages. – I

☐ The school currently only has one method of dealing with troublesome students. – S

Exercise C

One of the following target audiences is the most suitable (MS) whilst another is the least suitable (LS):

☐ Trainee teachers – LS

☐ Students at the school

☐ The head teacher/leadership team – MS

☐ Parents of students at the school

THE QTS
NUMERACY
SKILLS TEST
INTRODUCTION

What is the QTS numeracy skills test?

The QTS numeracy skills test is an assessment of your numeracy skills. In other words, it tests your ability to do mathematics. You need to pass the numeracy test in order to begin teacher training.

The QTS numeracy skills test is similar to the literacy test in a number of ways. It is taken on a computer at a Learndirect centre and your first attempt is free of charge. Unlike the literacy test, which takes around 45 minutes to complete, you are given 48 minutes to complete the numeracy skills test. It may appear daunting, but with the right guidance, the numeracy skills test can be overcome.

What am I being tested on?

The numeracy skills test is divided into two parts. The first section focuses on mental arithmetic, whilst the second features written arithmetic and data. Both sections cover a number of areas, including:

Addition	Subtraction	Multiplication	Division
Fractions	Time	Measurements	Conversions
Decimals	Percentages	Proportions	Ratio

There are a few differences between the two sections, but their content is generally quite similar; the skills you learn for one section will be applicable for the other. The content in this part of the book will be divided into a section on general numeracy knowledge, followed by sections on mental arithmetic and written arithmetic. The final two sections will include practice questions. General tips for each section will also be given.

What is the pass mark?

The pass mark for the numeracy skills test is 63%, and the test contains 28 questions. This means that you need to answer at least 18 of the questions correctly in order to pass. Each question is worth one mark. There are 12 questions in the mental arithmetic section of the test, and 16 questions in the written arithmetic section. Although there are more marks available for the second section of the numeracy skills test, it is important that you devote plenty of time to both parts since you can't be sure what questions will be asked. It's better to learn everything rather than only learn a few things, only to have them not show up!

Why is the test important?

The numeracy skills test is important because it gauges your ability to perform numerical tasks which will be vital for a teacher. Even if you don't plan on becoming a maths or science teacher, mathematical skills are necessary for a number of everyday and teaching activities. For example, all teachers will be required to mark work, which involves addition. This might also involve converting a mark into a percentage, which involves the conversion skill. A teacher will also be required to construct lesson plans, which may involve calculating time. Essentially, teaching requires a strong understanding of a few general mathematical areas, and so the QTS numeracy skills test is used to make sure you are up to the task.

How can I prepare for the test?

A lot of the skills required to pass the numeracy skills test will have been gained in everyday life. It is likely that you've made conversions from fractions to percentages before, and that you've got a decent grasp of measurements such as distance, money and time. However, you can't rely on your everyday experiences alone in order to pass the test, and some extra preparation is absolutely essential.

The best way to prepare for the numeracy skills test is to use the resources in this book to identify your strengths and weaknesses. Go through each section and try to answer the sample questions – you'll quickly find out which types of question you are comfortable with and which you struggle with.

How should I use this book?

The next chapter will cover the general skills required to answer questions in both sections of the QTS numeracy skills test. Read through the explanation and tips for each area, and then give the sample questions a go. Once you're confident about your ability in each area, attempt the mock test. This will give you an idea of where you are currently at and what you need to do next in order to achieve the highest marks possible.

THE QTS
NUMERACY
SKILLS TEST
GENERAL SKILLS

Introduction

In this chapter, you will have the opportunity to look at the key techniques required to pass the QTS numeracy skills test. These include conversions of all kinds, as well as the calculation of fractions, percentages, and more. The skills that you learn in this chapter will serve you for both the mental arithmetic and written arithmetic sections of the numeracy skills test, so this chapter is vital if you aren't entirely confident in your maths ability.

Fractions

One of the most important skills that you'll need is the ability to work with fractions, and understand how to simplify them. To simplify a fraction, you need to find the lowest possible denominator. In other words, you need to find a number which both the top number (numerator) and bottom number (denominator) will divide into whilst still being whole numbers. For example:

$$\frac{5}{20}$$

This fraction can be simplified because both 5 and 20 are divisible by 5:

$$\frac{5}{20} = \frac{1}{4}$$

However, not all fractions can be simplified so neatly. For example:

$$\frac{7}{15}$$

This cannot be simplified any further because 7 is a prime number. This means that it is only divisible by 1 and itself (7). 15 is divisible by 1, 3, 5 and itself (15). Since dividing by 1 won't simplify the fraction any further, and there are no other numbers which both 7 and 15 are divisible by, this fraction is as simple as it can be. Simplification of fractions might not appear on its own as a question topic, but it will be vital for most questions which include fractions.

Many people find fractions to be rather tricky, especially when multiplying or dividing them. The easiest way to multiply fractions is as follows:

$$\frac{3}{5} \times \frac{2}{6}$$

1. Multiply the top two numbers: $3 \times 2 = 6$

2. Multiply the bottom two numbers: $5 \times 6 = 3$

3. Insert the two new figures into the fraction: $\frac{6}{30}$

4. Simplify the fraction: $\frac{6}{30} = \frac{1}{5}$

    = Simplify the fraction as much as possible: $630 = 15$

Dividing fractions is slightly more complicated. The best way to divide two fractions is to swap the two digits of the second fraction around:

$$\frac{3}{5} \div \frac{2}{6} = \frac{3}{5} \div \frac{6}{2}$$

Then, turn the division operation into a multiplication, then carry on as though it were an ordinary fraction multiplication:

$$\frac{3}{5} \times \frac{6}{2} = \frac{18}{10}$$

Currently, this is an improper fraction. It needs to be simplified:

$$\frac{18}{10} = \frac{9}{5} = 1\frac{4}{5}$$

For addition of fractions, you need to make sure that the denominator is the same. This may involve simplification. In this example, the first fraction has been multiplied by 6, and the second by 5. After that, the top two numbers are added together:

$$\frac{3}{5} + \frac{2}{6} = \frac{18}{30} + \frac{10}{30} = \frac{28}{30}$$

Then, all that's needed is to simplify the final fraction:

$$\frac{28}{30} = \frac{14}{15}$$

For subtraction, the exact same process is followed, but by subtracting the top two numbers rather than adding them together.

Decimals

The key to solving questions with decimals is to keep track of decimal places. Place value completely affects the value of the decimal, so keep a close eye on the decimal places whenever you perform an operation using decimals.

When multiplying or dividing decimals, you will need to move them spaces either to the left or the right. If you multiply, the decimal point will move to the right.

$$0.008 \times 10 = 0.08$$
$$0.008 \times 100 = 0.8$$
$$0.008 \times 1000 = 8$$

Conversely, dividing will move the decimal point to the left.

$$0.008 \div 10 = 0.0008$$
$$0.008 \div 100 = 0.00008$$
$$0.008 \div 1000 = 0.000008$$

There are two different ways of multiplying decimals effectively. One relies on knowledge of decimals and decimal places, whilst the other uses fractions:

$$0.6 \times 0.9$$

The first way to solve this is to ignore the decimal points and perform a multiplication:

$$6 \times 9 = 54$$

Then, add the 2 decimals to the figure (one for 0.6 and one for 0.9). 54 then becomes **0.54**.

Alternatively, you can convert the decimals into fractions. All decimals have a denominator of 10:

$$0.6 \times 0.9 = \frac{6}{10} \times \frac{9}{10} = \frac{54}{100} = 54 \div 100 = 0.54$$

As you can see, both methods are effective in multiplying decimals. Use whichever you feel most comfortable with.

For adding and subtracting decimals, the process is much simpler. You simply need to make sure that the decimal points match:

$$5.56 + 7.871 = 13.431$$

Percentages

The term 'per cent' means 'per one-hundred'. This means that whatever figure comes before the percentage symbol (%) is out of 100. For example, say that a text noted that 25% of students failed to wear the correct school uniform. It could also be said that, for every 100 students, 25 of them fail to wear correct school uniform. This number can then be manipulated to better represent the total number of students. If there are 200 students in the school, then 50 students fail to wear correct school uniform (since 50 is 25% of 200).

Say that the following question was asked:

20% of students in the school fail to wear correct school uniform. There are 200 students in the school. How many students fail to wear correct school uniform?

There are a few ways which would lead you to the correct answer:

a) multiply 100 by 2 to get 200 (the number of students in the school) and then multiply 20 by 2 accordingly to get **40**.

b) change 20% into a decimal (0.2), then multiply it by 200 to get **40**.

c) recognise that 20% is the same as saying 1/5, and then dividing 200 by 5 to come to **40**.

d) divide 100 by 20 to get 5, then divide 200 by 5 to get 20% of 200, which is **40**.

Different methods work better for different people, although these have been ordered in terms of simplicity and general efficiency. The first method likely takes the least effort to come to, but nevertheless it's helpful to know that there are several ways of getting the correct answer when it comes to figuring out a percentage.

It's likely that you will also be asked to convert percentages into fractions or decimals (or vice versa). To convert a fraction to a percentage, you must do the following:

$$\frac{8}{10} = 8 \div 10 = 0.8$$

$$0.8 \times 100 = 80 \ (80\%)$$

Converting a decimal to a percentage is much simpler, since all decimals are out of 100, the same as a percentage. This means that you take the digits behind the decimal point and turn them into the percentage:

$$0.5 = 50\%$$
$$0.33 = 33\%$$
$$0.78 = 78\%$$

Averages

There are a few different types of average which appear in the numeracy skills test. This section will cover how to find all of them.

The **mode** is the most common figure in a set of numbers. For example:

$$3, 3, 3, 1, 5, 7, 4, 4, 2, 2, 8, 9.$$

In this set of values, the most common to occur is 3. Therefore, the mode of this set of numbers is 3.

The **mean** is another form of average which requires you to add all the values together, and then divide this new figure by the number of values in the set:

$$\frac{3 + 3 + 3 + 1 + 5 + 7 + 4 + 4 + 2 + 2 + 8 + 9}{12} = 4.25$$

The **median** is the figure which appears in the middle of a set when the numbers are placed in order. Using the same numbers as above, see the following example:

1, 2, 2, 3, 3, 3, 4, 4, 5, 7, 8, 9.

In this case, there is no single middle number. For sets like this, take the two middle numbers, and take a mean from them:

$$\frac{3 + 4}{2} = 3.5$$

So, the median for this set of numbers is **3.5**.

Finally, the **range** is an averaged derived by calculating the difference between the highest and lowest values. Using the same set of numbers as before, subtract the lowest value from the highest value to get the range:

$$9 - 1 = 8$$

In the test, it is possible that you will be asked to derive any or all of these kinds of average from a set of numbers. For this reason, you need to make sure that you are comfortable with all of them.

THE QTS NUMERACY SKILLS TEST
MENTAL ARITHMETIC

Introduction

This chapter will cover the mental arithmetic section of the QTS numeracy skills test. In this chapter, you will learn what kind of questions are asked, how these questions are presented and how to answer them.

How is this section presented?

The mental arithmetic part of the QTS numeracy skills test is the first section which you will face. As previously mentioned, there are twelve questions in this section, coming to a total of twelve marks available. Given that the pass mark for the entire test is eighteen marks, scoring well on the mental arithmetic section can put you in an excellent position for the written arithmetic questions. If you happened to score full marks on the mental arithmetic section, you would only need to answer one third of the written arithmetic questions correctly in order to pass the entire test. Despite this, remember to take both sections seriously while studying for the numeracy skills test. Putting all of your eggs in one basket is incredibly risky.

In the mental arithmetic portion of the test, you will listen to the twelve questions through a pair of headphones. For each question, you are given eighteen seconds to give your answer. During this time, the question is read out twice. After the allotted time has passed, the next question will play and you will be unable to return to the previous question.

The aim of this section is to assess how well you can perform mental arithmetic calculations. This means that calculators are not allowed, although you may take note of numbers in order to assist your working.

General tips for mental arithmetic

When the question is read for the first time, take the opportunity to take note of all the relevant information. Don't write down the whole question – just the numbers and key information that you're going to be working with. For example, if a question asks you to convert one or more numbers from decimals to fractions, note down all of the numbers, whether they are decimals or fractions, and then the function you need to perform (conversion). By doing this, you have all of the information ready to answer the question. If you miss any of the details, do not panic. You have a second reading of the question which can help you pick up on the rest of the information.

Once you're ready to answer the question, get to it immediately. You don't have a lot of time to solve the question, so try not to waste any time once you know that you have all of the information you need. However, try not to panic due to the time constraints – the questions are designed so that they are meant to be answerable during the allotted time.

Try not to leave any questions blank when answering this section. If you're not sure about what the answer is, it is better to write an educated guess and possibly get it right, rather than leave the question blank. For example, you may be stuck choosing between two possible answers for a single question. Of course, only one of them can be correct, but it's important that you choose one and enter it. Do not attempt to give multiple answers for the same question; you can't hedge your bets like that.

If you are completely clueless about an answer, it's still better to give something than nothing. Since you can't return to the questions later, you may as well fill in every answer with something, even if it's wrong. At worst, you don't get the mark – which you wouldn't have got anyway if you had left the space blank – but at best you could stumble upon the correct answer, and this could reward you with a point. However, you shouldn't rely on guesswork to get you through the QTS numeracy skills test – accurate answers as the result of practice are what will allow you to pass.

Finally, don't allow yourself to get too worried if you're on a streak of incorrect or unsure answers. It may be the case that the questions are simply quite difficult for everyone, and there will be some questions that you understand better later on. If worst comes to worst, there's still the written section of the numeracy skills test to earn some marks back with.

Mental Arithmetic – Practice Questions

This section includes a number of questions which cover all of the areas featured in the mental arithmetic section of the QTS numeracy skills test. Use these to familiarise yourself with the style of question being asked. When you're ready, pick 12 questions at random and attempt them for yourself. Time yourself for each question. Since you will only have eighteen seconds to answer each question in the real test, aim to answer each of these practice questions within that same timeframe.

1.

There are 30 pupils in a class. 6 pupils have been moved from the bottom group of Literacy to the top group of Literacy. What percentage of pupils have been moved up?

Answer

2.

120 students took part in an online test. 10% of students failed to achieve a C grade. How many students failed to achieve a C grade?

Answer

3.

65 pupils took part in sports day. There are 150 pupils who attend that school. What is the fraction of pupils that took part in sports day over the number of pupils who attend that school? Give your answer in its lowest terms.

Answer

4.

There are 220 pupils at a secondary school. A quarter of students achieved A-C grades in the year 2015. How many students did not achieve an A-C grade?

Answer

5.

A school has 3 classes going on a school trip in the same day. The school has 390 students. Each class has 30 students. What is the fraction of students that will still be at school that day? Give your answer in its lowest terms.

Answer

6.

There are 56 students in a class. 7 students received an award for their mathematics work. What is the fraction of students who received an award in that class? Give your answer in its lowest terms.

Answer

7.

A school arranges a bike marathon. 120 pupils take part. 1/6 of pupils finish the race in under half an hour. How many pupils did not finish the race in under half an hour?

Answer

8.

A school arranges a school trip to a theme park. There are 80 pupils attending the school trip. The ratio of children to adults is 5:1. How many adults will be needed for the trip to accommodate all the pupils?

Answer

9.

A class has 32 pupils. 10 pupils are struggling to meet the criteria in terms of their grades. What fraction of the class are not struggling with their grades? Give your answer in its lowest terms.

Answer

10.

260 pupils sat a GCSE English exam. The fraction of pupils who get a C grade or above is 3/4. How many pupils get Grade D or below?

Answer

11.

A school event consists of 13 tasks. Each task takes approximately 15 minutes. How long will the team event last? Give your answer in hours and minutes.

Answer

12.

A charity event is taking place at a local school. The event consists of 6 smaller events per day. The event lasts for 3 days. Each event is 20 minutes long. In total, how many hours will the whole charity event take?

Answer

13.

In a school day, there are 5 lessons. Each lesson is 50 minutes long. How long are students in lessons for per day? Give your answer in hours and minutes.

Answer

14.

A P.E lesson lasts for 50 minutes. Students have 3 P.E lessons a week. How many hours are students in P.E lessons over 6 weeks?

Answer

15.

In an hour's science lesson, the teacher introduces 3 tasks, which the students must complete before the end of the lesson. The first task should take 15 minutes, the second task should take 20 minutes and the third task should take 20 minutes. How many minutes are left before the end of the lesson?

Answer

16.

Students are sat in their GCSE English examination. It's a 2-hour long exam. There are 2 sections to the exam. Planning takes approximately 10 minutes per section. There are 5 questions to answer in each section. If the student was to divide their time evenly for each question, how many minutes per question would they have? Deduct the planning time.

Answer

17.

A student is given 3 tasks for the day. Each task is 25 minutes long. In total, how long will it take for the student to complete the 3 tasks? Give your answer in hours and minutes.

Answer

18.

A school detention lasts an hour. A student has 4 sets of homework to complete. How long approximately does he have for each set of homework, if he were to complete all of his homework in one detention?

Answer

19.

A local school is having their sports day. Sports day consists of 12 sporting events. Each event takes approximately 20 minutes. In total, how long will sports day last? Give your answer in hours and minutes.

Answer

20.

A local school has introduced the Chinese language to their academic criteria. They are going to teach the lesson twice a week. Each lesson is 45 minutes long. How many hours will students be learning Chinese over 6 weeks?

Answer

21.

A primary school has a total of 360 pupils. In total, 85 pupils suffer with learning difficulties. What is the percentage of pupils who suffer with learning difficulties? Convert your answer into a decimal.

Answer

22.

A primary school has 80 pupils in Year 4. 12 pupils have a reading age that is below their actual age. What is the percentage of pupils who have a reading age that is below their actual age? Give your answer as a decimal.

Answer

23.

A secondary school has a total of 450 students. 132 students have entered the cross country fun run. What is the percentage of the number of students taking part in the cross country run? Give your answer as a decimal.

Answer

24.

Year Six has 130 pupils. 42 pupils last year were put on a school report to monitor their behaviour. What is the percentage of the number of pupils who are not on school reports? Give your answer as a decimal, and to two decimal places.

Answer

25.

A primary school has 80 pupils in Year Five. 20 pupils have been calculated to have attendance below the border line of school expectations. What is the percentage of pupils that are under the border line with regards to their attendance? Give your answer as a decimal.

Answer

Mental Arithmetic – Answers

1. 20%

Explanation: $\frac{6}{30} = \frac{1}{5} = \frac{20}{100} = $ 20%

2. 12

Explanation: 120 ÷ 10 = 12

3. 13/30

Explanation: 65 and 150 are both divisible by 5, resulting in 13 and 30 respectively.

4. 165

Explanation: One quarter of 220 is the same as dividing 220 by 4. This comes to 55. Subtract 55 from 220 to get 165.

5. 10/13

Explanation: 30 students in each class equals 90. So the number of students remaining at school is 300 $= \frac{300}{390}$ is divisible by 30.

6. 1/8

Explanation: Both 7 and 56 are divisible by 7, which equals 1 and 8 respectively.

7. 100

Explanation: 120 ÷ 6 = 20.   120 - 20 = 100.

8. 16

Explanation: For every 5 children, there must be one adult. So, divide 80 by 5 to get 16 (the number of adults needed).

9. 11/16

Explanation: 32 - 10 = 22. $\frac{22}{32}$ can be simplified to $\frac{11}{16}$ since 22 and 32 are both divisible by 2.

10. 65

Explanation: One quarter of 260 is the same as saying 260÷4=65.

11. 3 hours, 15 minutes

Explanation: 13 x 15=195 minutes. There are 60 minutes to each hour, so 180 minutes is 3 hours. Then just add the final 15 minutes.

12. 6 hours

Explanation: 20 x 6=120 minutes. 120 minutes is the equivalent of 2 hours. Multiply 2 x 3 (because the event lasts 3 days) to get a total of 6 hours across the whole event.

13. 4 hours and 10 minutes

Explanation: 50 x 5=250 minutes. 250 minutes = 4 hours and 10 minutes.

14. 15 hours

Explanation: 50 x 3=150 minutes. 150 x 6=900 minutes. 900÷60=15 hours. ..

15. 5 minutes

Explanation: 15+20+20=55 minutes. 60-55=5 minutes.

16. 10 minutes

Explanation: 2 hours divided by 2 sections equals 1 hour per section. So, 60 minutes minus 10 minutes (the time needed for planning per section) equals 50 minutes. 50 divided by 5 (the number of questions) equals 10 minutes.

17. 1 hour and 15 minutes

Explanation: 3 x 25=75 minutes. 75 minutes is the equivalent of 1 hour and 15 minutes since there are 60 minutes in an hour.

18. 15 minutes

Explanation: 60÷4=15 minutes.

19. 4 hours

Explanation: 12 x 20=240 minutes. Since there are 60 minutes in an hour, this means that 240 minutes equals 4 hours (or: 240÷60=4).

20. 9 hours

Explanation: 45 x 2=90 minutes. 90 x 6=540 minutes. 540÷60=9 hours.

21. 0.23

Explanation: 85÷360=0.23

22. 0.15

Explanation: 12 is 15% of 80. Then, to convert it to a decimal you simply move the decimal point 2 spaces to the left.

23. 0.29

Explanation: 132÷450=0.29

24. 0.67

Explanation: 88÷130=0.68

25. 0.25

Explanation: 20÷80=0.25

Conclusion

The mental arithmetic section of the QTS numeracy skills test can be quite tricky due to the short space of time allowed to answer each question. The trick is not to panic. Instead, focus on the vital information in each question. Remember that the questions are designed to be answerable in the given time-frame, so it certainly isn't impossible to do excellently in this section.

When you're confident about the mental arithmetic section, turn over to learn more about the written arithmetic part of the QTS numeracy skills test. Alternatively, head straight over to the mock test for even more practice questions.

THE QTS NUMERACY SKILLS TEST

WRITTEN ARITHMETIC

Introduction

This chapter will handle the written arithmetic section of the QTS numeracy skills test. We will follow on from the information given in the previous two chapters, so it is best to read those first to make sure that you haven't missed key tips. In this chapter, you will learn how the written arithmetic section of the test is presented, as well as some general tips. Finally, you will have the opportunity to read some sample questions, familiarise yourself with their format, and then answer them for yourself.

Once you feel confident about this section of the test, feel free to attempt the written arithmetic section of the mock test found at the end of this chapter.

How is this section presented?

The written arithmetic section is taken at a computer, and you are given 36 minutes to complete it. There is a total of sixteen questions in the written arithmetic section of the test, making it contribute significantly to the total marks of the paper. If you achieved full marks on this section, you would be well on your way to passing the test overall. For this reason, making sure that you can answer all the questions is very important.

Questions in this section can be presented in several different ways. Some questions will be given in a multiple-choice format, requiring you to pick a single or multiple answers. Others will ask for you to click on visualisations such as graphs to answer the question.

Generally, 7 questions in this section of the test will require you to interpret some data. The remaining 9 questions will be focused on mathematical reasoning.

Unlike the mental arithmetic section, the written arithmetic section of the numeracy skills test will allow for the use of a calculator, which will appear on screen. While you might think this will make the section easier, it is important to remember that the calculator won't bring you straight to the answer – you will still need to do some working out on your own.

General tips for written arithmetic

Unlike the mental arithmetic section, the written section allows for you to return to questions, so long as you have time. Use this to your advantage. This allows you to skip any questions that you are struggling with, and return to them later if you have time. By doing this, you can secure marks on the questions that you find more manageable rather than getting stuck on a tougher one. Since each question is worth the same amount as any other, you should prioritise questions that you find easiest to answer before moving onto something trickier. This way, you can make sure that you've secured as many marks as possible.

Remember that you only have 36 minutes to answer the sixteen questions in this section. This means that you have 2 minutes and 15 seconds for each question. Keep an eye on the time but also try not to rush, since you could end up making mistakes. Striking a balance is vital. The questions here are more complex than in the mental arithmetic section, so take the time to read all the information given. Since the information is available on-screen and not played through headphones, you should take your time and make sure that you answer the questions properly. However, make sure you keep to the time constraints – spending too long on a single question will mean that you'll have to catch up later!

Also, make sure that you are aware of what kind of question you are answering. Different questions will ask you to answer in different ways (e.g. multiple-choice, multiple-response, single-response), so read the instructions for each question carefully.

Using BIDMAS

Since the questions will take longer to figure out than in the mental arithmetic section, it may be required to take your answer in steps, using multiple different functions. For questions like this, use the BIDMAS technique to make sure that you perform the functions in the correct order.

BIDMAS is the order in which you should do all the functions in any question. The order is as follows:

Brackets	Firstly, you should do any of the question which happens to be in brackets.
Indices	Indices (or 'powers of') should be performed second. These probably won't show up in the numeracy skills test.
Division	The division function should be performed third.
Multiplication	This comes after division.
Addition	Addition should always come before subtraction
Subtraction	Finally, do any subtraction tasks as necessary.

It may seem trivial, but the order you perform functions can drastically affect the outcome of a question. For example:

$$2 + 2 - 2 \times 6$$

If BIDMAS is followed, then you perform the multiplication first (2 x 6), bringing you to 12. Then, you do the addition (2 + 2) which equals four. Then, you would do the subtraction (4 - 12), which brings you to an answer of -8.

If BIDMAS is not followed, the answer can be completely different. For example, perform the functions in the order that they are shown in the sum. First, you'd do the addition (2 + 2 = 4), followed by the subtraction (4 - 2 = 2). Finally, you would perform the multiplication (2 x 6), bringing you to 12. This is a completely different answer, and would be considered incorrect in the numeracy skills test. Therefore, you must follow BIDMAS as it is the rule that all questions will have been written by.

BIDMAS can also be a useful technique for structuring your thoughts when answering one of the questions. This means that if you get lost in thought, you can recall the last operation you did and then continue from there. This means that you'll be able to continue from where you left off.

Using the Calculator

As previously mentioned, the written arithmetic section of the numeracy skills test allows you to use a calculator. This calculator appears on-screen (you cannot bring and use your own) and it is basic – it isn't a scientific calculator by any means. For this reason, you won't be able to solve every question solely using the calculator. However, this doesn't stop it from being incredibly useful for some questions.

The calculator can be operated by either clicking on numbers with the mouse or by using the number pad on the right-hand side of your keyboard. The 'Num Lock' key must be pressed to activate it first. The keyboard you use may have a green light to show whether the number pad is activated or not.

Remember that there are two separate 'clear' functions, and they are used for different reasons. C is used to completely clear all operations on the calculator; this should be used after finishing a calculation and moving onto a new one, such as the next stage of the question or a whole new question. CE is used to cancel the last operation. For example, say that you had the following sum to complete

$$(4 \times 2) \times 8$$

Say that you have just completed the first calculation (4 x 2), coming to 8. Then, instead of typing 8 for the second operation (8 x 8), you accidentally hit 8 twice, reading 88. Pressing CE will clear the current operation, giving you an opportunity to type 8 again without having to restart the whole process. This can only be used before you complete the operation (i.e. before you press the '=' button).

It cannot be stressed enough that the calculator cannot pass the numeracy skills test for you, so don't rely on it constantly. Use it where appropriate to get your answers, but be prepared to do some working out of your own.

Written Arithmetic – Practice Questions

Now that you've read about the written arithmetic section of the numeracy skills test, use these practice questions to get an idea for what you might face in the real thing. This section is divided into questions on interpreting data as well as general arithmetic. You are allowed to use a calculator for this section. Attempt some of the questions, then head over to the answers section to see where you've done well, as well as where you need to improve.

Interpreting Data

1.

The set of data below shows the result in a year 7 P.E test for 45 pupils. The marks are out of 15. The teacher wants to find the mean mark for this test. Give your answer to 1 decimal place.

P.E test marks	No. of pupils	No. of pupils X P.E test mark
1	0	1 X 0 = 0
2	0	2 X 0 = 0
3	4	
4	1	
5	3	
6	1	
7	2	
8	6	
9	3	
10	4	
11	5	
12	6	
13	5	
14	2	
15	3	
Totals		

The mean mark is:

2.

The two-way table shown compares results for Maths Test 1 and Maths Test 2.

Maths Test 1	Maths Test 2								Total
	A*	A	B	C	D	E	F	U	
A*									
A									
B		1	1		1				3
C			2	2	12	1			17
D				5	3	3			11
E				4			1	1	6
F									
U									
Total		1	3	11	16	4	1	1	37

(1) The number of pupils' who achieved a C grade in both the Maths Test 1 and Maths Test 2 is 12. True or false?

(2) The number of pupils who achieved a B grade in the Maths Test 2 is 11. True or false?

(3) The percentage number of pupils who achieved a C grade or above in Maths Test 2 is approximately 84%. True or false?

3.

Test grades in History, Geography, Media and English for Year 11 are compared by box-and-whisker diagrams shown below. Grades in percentages are shown on the vertical axis.

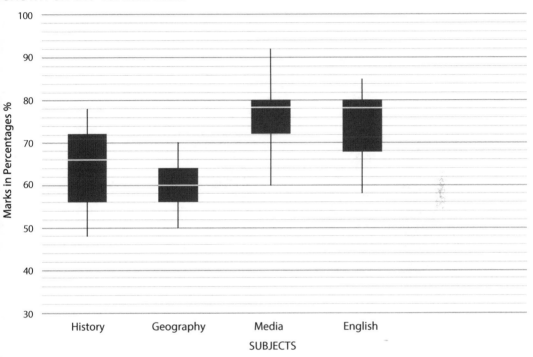

(1) The median range is the same in Media and English. True or false?

(2) Media is Year 11's strongest subject. True or false?

(3) The interquartile range of Media is higher than that of Geography. True or false?

4.

Pupils receive their Geography mock test results and are compared by three box-and-whisker diagrams shown below. Marks out of 100 are shown on the vertical axis.

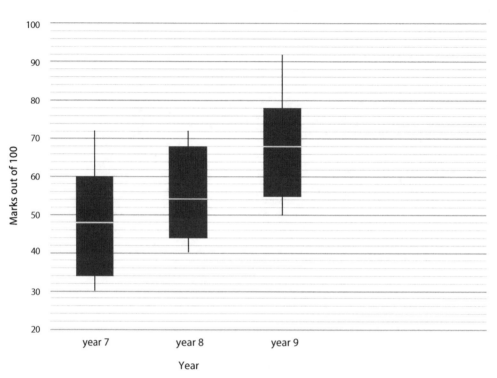

(1) The interquartile range for Year 7 is lower than the interquartile range of Year 8. True or false?

(2) The highest mark for Year 8 was 68. True or false?

(3) The difference in the median mark for Year 9 is approximately 20 marks more than Year 7. True or false?

5.

A teacher represents the relationship between marks in a pop quiz for English Literature and a pop quiz in English Language by the scatter graph shown below. The English Literature test is out of 20, and the English Language test is out of 30. Indicate all true statements below:

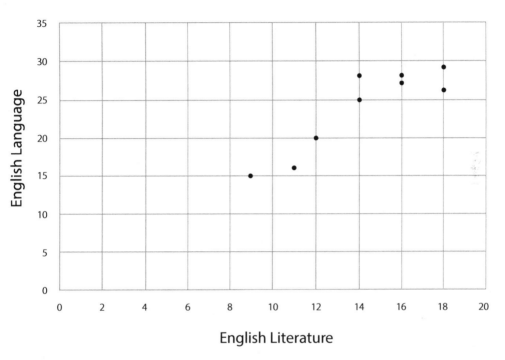

(1) In general, the higher the mark in English Literature, the higher the mark in English Language. True or false?

(2) The lowest mark in English Language was 9. True or false?

(3) The highest mark in English Literature was 18. True or false?

6.

A teacher represents the relationship between marks in a Media Studies test and a Film Studies test by the scatter graph shown below. The Media studies test is out of 60, and the Film studies test is out of 50. Indicate all true statements below:

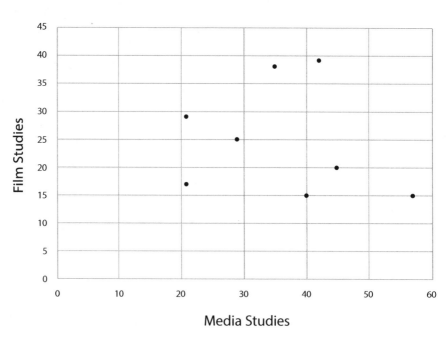

(1) There is no correlation between the Media and Film studies grades. True or false?

(2) When the pupil's mark in Film Studies was 25, there mark in Media Studies was 30. True or false?

(3) The mean mark for Media studies was approximately 36.25. True or false?

7.

The grades were recorded for a Dance performance for 45 pupils. The data is shown on a cumulative frequency diagram below. Indicate all true statements below:

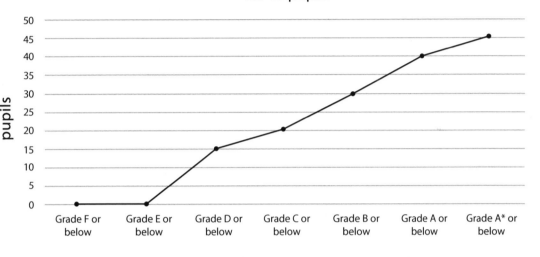

The grades were recorded for a Dance performance for 45 pupils

(1) 15 pupils got a Grade D or below. True or false?

(2) Over half the pupils got a got a Grade B or above. True or false?

(3) 30 pupils received a B grade or below. True or false?

8.

Grades based on English homework were recorded for 50 pupils. The data is shown on a cumulative frequency diagram below. Indicate all true statements below:

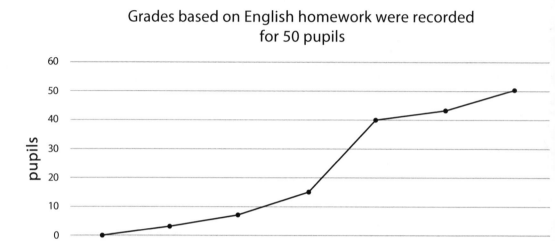

Grades based on English homework were recorded for 50 pupils

(1) 1 pupil received a Grade F or below. True or false?

(2) 10 pupils received a Grade B or above. True or false?

(3) 70% of pupils received a C Grade or above. True or false?

9.

Pupils who were put on a school report for lateness were analysed between 2005 and 2010.

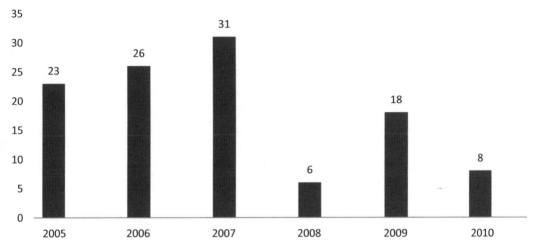

(1) The total number of pupils who were put on a school report for lateness between 2007 and 2009 is 54. True or false?

(2) The difference between 2005 and 2007 regarding how many pupils were put on a school report is 8. True or false?

(3) The mean from 2008 to 2010 is 8. True or false?

10.

A teacher represents the relationship between marks in a Maths test and a Science test by the scatter graph shown below. The Maths test is out of 100, and the Science test is also out of 100. Indicate all true statements below:

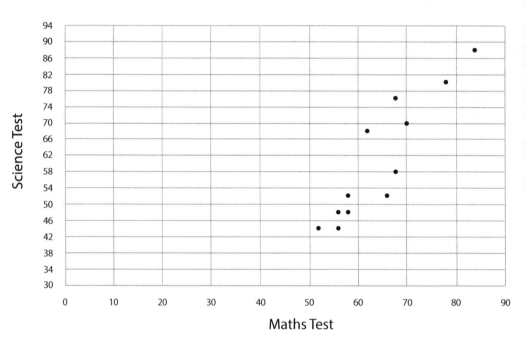

(1) In general, if a pupil's mark was high in Science it was also high in Maths. True or false?

(2) The correlation between Maths and Science marks in this test was negative. True or false?

(3) When the pupil's mark in Maths was 70, the corresponding mark in Science was also 70. True or false?

Numerical Reasoning

1.

Two classes are put together in the morning. Each class has 25 pupils. One class has 7 pupils that are vegetarian. The other class has 5 people that are vegetarian. In total, what is the percentage of the number of pupils that are vegetarian?

Answer

2.

What is 70% of £120?

Answer

3.

What is 61% of £578?

Answer

4.

What is 11.5% of £990?

Answer

5.

A secondary school has 3 school trips on the same day. In total, there are 480 students who attend that secondary school. 3/8 of pupil are on school trips. How many students will not be going on a school trip?

Answer

6.

A football tournament is taking place at a local secondary school. In total, there are 108 pupils taking part. Each team has 12 members. There are 4 football courts. How many teams can play at the same time?

Answer

7.

3/8 of girls play football for the school team. 2/5 of boys play football for the school team. What is the total fraction of pupils who play football for the school team?

Answer

8.

8 pupils from a school took the 11 plus test to get into a grammar school. Their marks were as follows. 69 52 49 71 63 70 70 69. What was the mean mark overall who took the 11 plus from that school?

Answer

9.

What is 1.8% of 10 millilitres?

Answer [   ]

10.

A Geography class have taken a short test. The teacher spends 6 minutes marking and 2 minutes checking over the tests. There are 23 pupils in the geography class. How long in hours and minutes does it take to mark the geography tests?

Answer [   ]

Written Arithmetic – Answers

Interpreting Data

1.

The set of data below shows the result in a year 7 P.E test for 45 pupils. The marks are out of 15. The teacher wants to find the mean mark for this test. Give your answer to 1 decimal place.

P.E test marks	No. of pupils	No. of pupils X P.E test mark
1	0	1 X 0 = 0
2	0	2 X 0 = 0
3	4	
4	1	
5	3	
6	1	
7	2	
8	6	
9	3	
10	4	
11	5	
12	6	
13	5	
14	2	
15	3	
Totals		

Answer: 9.6

Explanation:

P.E test marks	No. of pupils	No. of pupils X P.E test mark
1	0	1 X 0 = 0
2	0	2 X 0 = 0
3	4	3 X 4 = 12
4	1	4 X 1 = 4
5	3	5 X 3 = 15
6	1	6 X 1 = 6
7	2	7 X 2 = 14
8	6	8 X 6 = 48
9	3	9 X 3 = 27
10	4	10 X 4 = 40
11	5	11 X 5 = 55
12	6	12 X 6 = 72
13	5	13 x 5 = 65
14	2	14 X 2 = 28
15	3	15 X 3 = 45
Totals	45	431

For this question, you need to multiply each of the marks by the number of students who got each mark (shown in right-hand column), coming to 431. Then, divide this by the number of students (45) to get 9.577777777777778. Round this up to 9.6 as the question requests.

2.

The two-way table shown compares results for Maths Test 1 and Maths Test 2.

Maths Test 1	Maths Test 2									
	A*	A	B	C	D	E	F	U		Total
A*										
A										
B	1	1		1						3
C		2	2	12	1					17
D			5	3	3					11
E			4			1	1			6
F										
U										
Total	1	3	11	16	4	1	1			37

(1) The number of pupils' who achieved a C grade in both the Maths Test 1 and Maths Test 2 is 12. True or false?

> True

(2) The number of pupils who achieved a B grade in the Maths Test 2 is 11. True or false?

> True

(3) The percentage number of pupils who achieved a C grade or above in Maths Test 2 is approximately 84%. True or false?

> True

3.

Test grades in History, Geography, Media and English for Year 11 are compared by box-and-whisker diagrams shown below. Grades in percentages are shown on the vertical axis.

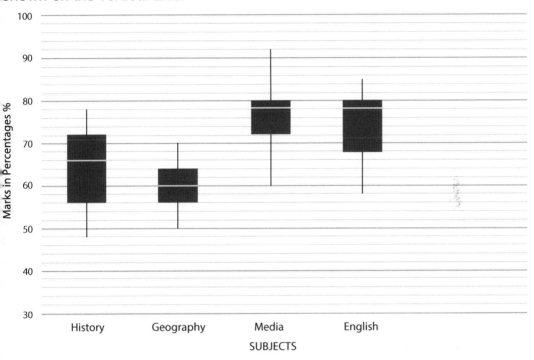

(1) The median range is the same in Media and English. True or false?

> True

(2) Media is Year 11's strongest subject. True or false?

> True

(3) The interquartile range of Media is higher than that of Geography. True or false?

> False

4.

Pupils receive their Geography mock test results and are compared by three box-and-whisker diagrams shown below. Marks out of 100 are shown on the vertical axis.

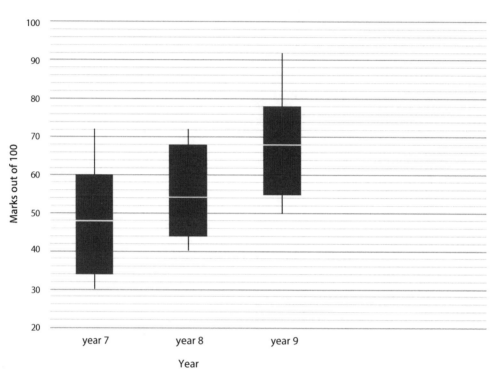

(1) The interquartile range for Year 7 is lower than the interquartile range of Year 8. True or false?

> False

(2) The highest mark for Year 8 was 68. True or false?

> False

(3) The difference in the median mark for Year 9 is approximately 20 marks more than Year 7. True or false?

> True

5.

A teacher represents the relationship between marks in a pop quiz for English Literature and a pop quiz in English Language by the scatter graph shown below. The English Literature test is out of 20, and the English Language test is out of 30. Indicate all true statements below:

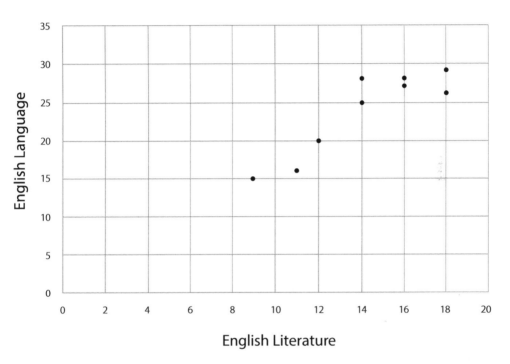

(1) In general, the higher the mark in English Literature, the higher the mark in English Language. True or false?

True

(2) The lowest mark in English Language was 9. True or false?

False

(3) The highest mark in English Literature was 18. True or false?

True

6.

A teacher represents the relationship between marks in a Media Studies test and a Film Studies test by the scatter graph shown below. The Media studies test is out of 60, and the Film studies test is out of 50. Indicate all true statements below:

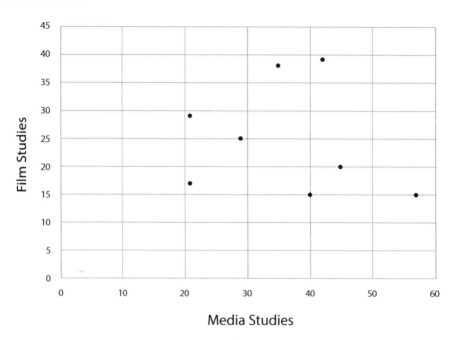

Media Studies

(1) There is no correlation between the Media and Film studies grades. True or false?

True

(2) When the pupil's mark in Film Studies was 25, there mark in Media Studies was 30. True or false?

False

(3) The mean mark for Media studies was approximately 36.25. True or false?

True

7.

The grades were recorded for a Dance performance for 45 pupils. The data is shown on a cumulative frequency diagram below. Indicate all true statements below:

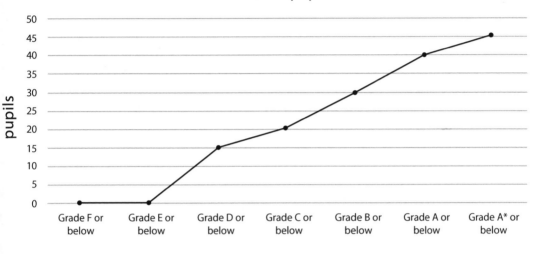

The grades were recorded for a Dance performance for 45 pupils

(1) 15 pupils got a Grade D or below. True or false?

True

(2) Over half the pupils got a got a Grade B or above. True or false?

False

(3) 30 pupils received a B grade or below. True or false?

True

8.

Grades based on English homework were recorded for 50 pupils. The data is shown on a cumulative frequency diagram below. Indicate all true statements below:

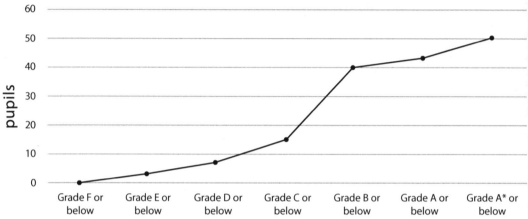

(1) 1 pupil received a Grade F or below. True or false?

False

(2) 10 pupils received a Grade B or above. True or false?

True

(3) 70% of pupils received a C Grade or above. True or false?

True

9.

Pupils who were put on a school report for lateness were analysed between 2005 and 2010.

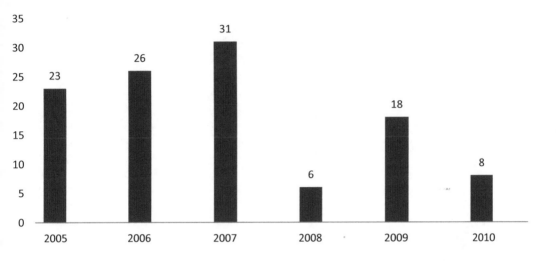

(1) The total number of pupils who were put on a school report for lateness between 2007 and 2009 is 54. True or false?

False

(2) The difference between 2005 and 2007 regarding how many pupils were put on a school report is 8. True or false?

True

(3) The mean from 2008 to 2010 is 8. True or false?

False

10.

A teacher represents the relationship between marks in a Maths test and a Science test by the scatter graph shown below. The Maths test is out of 100, and the Science test is also out of 100. Indicate all true statements below:

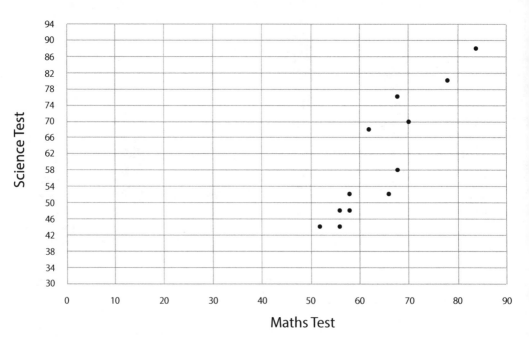

(1) In general, if a pupil's mark was high in Science it was also high in Maths. True or false?

True

(2) The correlation between Maths and Science marks in this test was negative. True or false?

False

(3) When the pupil's mark in Maths was 70, the corresponding mark in Science was also 70. True or false?

True

Numerical Reasoning

1. 24%

Explanation: Add the two classes of 25 together to get 50. Then, add 7 and 5 together to get 12. Multiply 50 by 2 to get 100 (100%) and then multiply 12 by 2 to get 24 (24%).

2. £84

Explanation: Using the calculator, divide £120 by 10 to get 10% of 120 (12). Then, multiply 10 by 7 to get 70% of 120 (84).

3. £352.58

Explanation: Start by dividing £578 by 10 to get 10% of 578 (57.8). Then, multiply 57.8 by 6 to get 60% of 578 (346.8). Hold onto this number. Separately, divide £578 by 100 to get 1% of 578 (5.78). Then, add 5.78 to 346.8 (1% + 60%) to get 61% of £578, which is £352.58.

Hint: Unless stated otherwise, it's a good idea to give your answer with two decimal places if possible (i.e. 352.58 rather than rounding up to 352.6).

4. £113.85

Explanation: Start by dividing £990 by 10 to get 10% of 990 (99). Hold onto this number. Separately, divide £990 by 100 to get 1% of 990 (9.9). Hold onto this number as well. Separately, divide £990 by 200 to get 0.5% of 990 (4.95). Then, add 4.95 and 9.9 to 99 (0.5% + 1% + 10% = 11.5%) to get 11.5% of £990 (£113.85).

5. 300

Explanation: Start by dividing 480 by 8 to get 60. This is $\frac{1}{8}$ of 480. Then multiply 60 by 3 to get $\frac{3}{8}$ of 480 (180). Then, subtract 180 from 480 to find out the number of students who would not be going on the school trip (300).

6. 8

Explanation: There are 4 courts, and each can have 2 teams playing on it at once. So, multiply 4 by 2 to get 8, which is the maximum number of teams which can play at the same time.

7. $\frac{31}{40}$

Explanation: Since the two fractions being dealt with have different denominators, they need to be changed. 40 is divisible by both 8 and 5, so it will become the new denominator. $\frac{3}{8} \times 5 = \frac{15}{40}$, and $\frac{2}{5} \times 8 = \frac{16}{40}$. Then, add $\frac{15}{40}$ to $\frac{16}{40}$ to get $\frac{31}{40}$. Since this fraction cannot be simplified any further, this is the final answer to the question.

8. 65.125

Explanation: This question is quite straight-forward when you have a calculator. Add all the figures together (69, 52, 49, 71, 63, 70, 70, 69) to get 513. Then, divide this by the number of values (8) to get 65.125.

9. 0.18

Explanation: Divide 1.8 by 10 to get 0.18. Remember to move all digits one place to the right, since 10 has one zero.

10. 3 hours and 4 minutes.

Explanation: Add 6 to 2 to get 8, the total amount of time that the teacher spends marking and checking each test. Then multiply 8 by 23 (the number of tests being marked). This comes to 184 minutes. Convert this into hours and minutes by dividing 180 by 60 to get 3 (3 hours) and then take the remaining 4 to get 3 hours and 4 minutes.

THE QTS
NUMERACY
SKILLS TEST
MOCK TEST

Introduction

Now that you're familiar with the content and style of the QTS numeracy skills test, it's time to attempt the mock test. Bear the following in mind before you begin:

- The total mark for this paper is 28: 12 marks in the mental arithmetic section, and 16 marks for the written arithmetic section. Each question is worth one mark.

- You have 48 minutes to complete the paper. 12 minutes should be spent on the mental arithmetic section, whilst the remaining 36 minutes is reserved for the written arithmetic section.

- For the mental arithmetic section, remember that you only have 18 seconds to answer each question. Try and answer these questions in this time.

- You cannot return to the mental arithmetic section once you have completed it, so make sure that you do this first under the time constraints to recreate the real test as accurately as possible.

- Also, remember that the real test will be computerised. If possible, try typing your answers at a computer to get a better feel for the real test.

Section 1 – Mental Arithmetic

1.

A school arranges a bike ride for students in order to raise money for a charity. The bike ride is 32 kilometres long. If 8km is approximately 5 miles, how many miles will the bike ride consist of?

Answer

2.

A school puts on a fun walk for students in the summer. A kilometre is equal to 1,000 metres. The walk is approximately 4,000 metres long. How many kilometres are the students going to walk?

Answer

3.

A class of 32 students has 12 boys. What is the ratio of boys to girls? Give your answer in its simplest form.

Answer

4.

What is 25% of 260 kilograms?

Answer

5.

What is 60% of 580 pounds?

Answer

6.

What is 45% of 190 kilometres?

Answer

7.

In a film studies lesson, the lesson is split into 3 sections. The first section will be a 10-minute planning section, the second section will be answering questions for 15 minutes and the last stage will be for filming. The lesson is 50 minutes long. How long do students get for the filming stage?

Answer

8.

A school disco is expecting 100 students to attend. For this event, they will need to supply drinks. Each drinking cup holds 250 millilitres. How many litres will be needed to fill the cups if all 100 students were to have 2 cups each?

Answer

9.

Convert 0.014% to a decimal.

Answer

10.

A student scored 55%, 63% and 71% in three different English tests. What was the student's mean mark?

Answer

11.

A school hall can accommodate 210 chairs. There are 48 students and 91 parents in a special awards ceremony. How many vacant seats are there?

Answer

12.

Two P.E classes are joint together. In one class, 1/6 of the pupils are female. In the other class, 5/12 of the pupils are female. Once combined, what is the total fraction for both classes that are female?

Answer

Section 2 – Written Arithmetic

Interpreting Data

1.

The set of data below shows the results of Year 10's height order. 32 pupils measured their height. The teacher wants to find the median height in her class. Give your answer to 1 decimal place.

Height (cm)	No. of pupils	No. of pupils X height (cm)
125	1	125 x 1 = 125
130	2	130 x 2 = 260
135	3	
140	2	
145	4	
150	5	
155	4	
160	4	
165	3	
170	2	
175	1	
180	1	
Totals		

2.

Maths GCSE grades were recorded for 40 pupils. The data is shown on a cumulative frequency diagram below. Indicate all true statements below:

Maths GCSE grades recorded for 40 pupils

(1) 15 pupils get above Grade C. True or false?

(2) 30 pupils get above Grade D. True or false?

(3) 50% of the 40 pupils get a C Grade or above. True or false?

3.

A teacher represents the relationship between marks in a P.E test and an English test by the scatter graph shown below. The P.E marks are out of 20 and the English marks are out of 60. Indicate all true statements below:

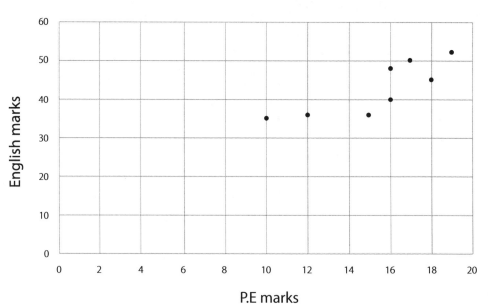

P.E marks

(1) When the pupil's mark in P.E was 18, their English mark was also 18. True or false?

(2) The correlation between English and P.E marks in this test was positive. True or false?

(3) In general, if the mark in P.E was high, their mark in English was also high. True or false?

Numerical Reasoning

1.

A school trip to the theatre is taking place. 16 teachers are supervising as well as 8 parents. In total, there are 24 supervisors. 3/6 of supervisors are male. How many supervisors are female?

Answer

2.

Two GCSE dance classes join. The total number of pupils in the class is 35. If 3/7 of the pupils were from one dance class, how many pupils were there from the second dance class?

Answer

3.

A film class of 31 have just sat a mock Exam. The exam has 2 sections – a short screening and 2 essays. It takes approximately 14 minutes to mark each exam. They also spend 4 minutes checking over the whole exam. How long in hours and minutes does it take to mark the Film mock exam?

Answer

4.

A Maths class have taken a short test. The teacher spends 9 minutes marking and 3 minutes checking over the tests. There are 35 pupils in the class. How long in hours does it take to mark the maths tests?

Answer

5.

What is 88.5% of 1,000 metres?

Answer

6.

For a Maths exam, 3/8 achieved the above and beyond award for great results. 4/12 in another Maths class achieved the above and beyond award. What is the total fraction of both exams combined that achieved the above and beyond award?

Answer

7.

The school day starts at 08.45. A pupil is running late by 100 minutes. What time will the pupil arrive at school?

Answer

8.

A skills challenge is taking place at a local secondary school. In total, 63 pupils take part. For every group, there are 3 boys to every 4 girls. How many groups would be needed to accommodate all 63 pupils?

Answer

9.

A pupil had three exams for his science GCSE. He scored 74% on exam 1, 86% on exam 2 and 65% on exam 3. What was the pupil's mean mark for his science GCSE?

Answer

THE QTS NUMERACY SKILLS TEST

MOCK TEST ANSWERS AND EXPLANATIONS

Introduction

Congratulations on completing the mock test. Take a look at the answers and see where you've done well, as well as where you need to improve.

If you haven't done as well as you'd hoped, don't panic! Read over your revision materials, take another look at the sample questions, then give the mock test another go later.

Section 1 – Mental Arithmetic

1. 20 miles

Explanation: 32 divided by 8 is 4. So, in order to get 8km to 32km, you need to multiply it by 4. Multiply 5 miles by 4 to get 20 miles, the equivalent of 32km.

2. 4

Explanation: 1,000 metres is the equivalent of 1km. Therefore, 4,000 metres must be the equivalent of 4km.

3. 3:5

Explanation: If the class of 32 has 12 boys, then the remaining 20 pupils must be girls. This means that the ratio of boys to girls is 12:20. However, this can be simplified. 12 and 20 are both divisible by 4. Divide 12 by 4 to get 3 and divide 20 by 4 to get 5. This produces the simplest form of the ratio – 3:5.

4. 65

Explanation: 25% is the equivalent of one quarter, which in turn is the equivalent of dividing 260 by 4. If it helps, divide 260 by 2 to get 130, and then divide by 2 again to get 65.

5. 348 pounds

Explanation: Start by dividing 580 by 10 to get 10% of 580 (58). Then, multiply 58 by 6 to get 60% of 580, which is 348.

6. 85.5

Explanation: Start by dividing 190 by 20 to get 5% of 190 (9.5). Then, multiply 9.5 by 9 to get 45% of 190 (85.5).

7. 25 minutes

Explanation: Add 10 to 15 to get 25 minutes. Then, subtract 25 minutes from 50 minutes to get 25 minutes.

8. 50

Explanation: Each of the 100 students is going to have 2 cups each. This means that 200 cups will be needed in total. Multiply 250 millilitres by 200 people to get 50,000ml. Since the question is asking how many litres will be needed, you then need to convert 50,000ml into litres. Since 1000ml = 1 litre, divide 50,000 by 1,000 to get 50 litres.

9. 0.00014

Explanation: Divide 0.014% by 100. This means moving the figure two decimal places to the right.

10. 63%

Explanation: Add 55, 63 and 71 together to get 189, then divide 189 by 3 to get the mean. It may help to break the division up into parts. First, divide 180 by 3 to get 60. Then, divide 9 by 3 to get 3. Add 60 to 3 to get 63.

11. 71

Explanation: Add 48 to 91 to get the total number of filled chairs in the room (139). Subtract 139 from 210 to get the number of vacant seats left over (71).

12. $\frac{7}{12}$

Explanation: Since the two fractions have different denominators, one will need to be changed to match the other. Multiply $\frac{1}{6}$ by 2 to get $\frac{2}{12}$. Then, add $\frac{2}{12}$ to $\frac{5}{12}$ to get $\frac{7}{12}$. This fraction cannot be simplified any further.

Section 2 – Written Arithmetic

Interpreting Data

1.

The set of data below shows the results of Year 10's height order. 32 pupils measured their height. The teacher wants to find the median height in her class. Give your answer to 1 decimal place.

Height (cm)	No. of pupils	No. of pupils X height (cm)
125	1	125 x 1 = 125
130	2	130 x 2 = 260
135	3	
140	2	
145	4	
150	5	
155	4	
160	4	
165	3	
170	2	
175	1	
180	1	
Totals		

Answer: 151.6cm

Height (cm)	No. of pupils.	No. of pupils X height (cm)
125	1	125 x 1 = 125
130	2	130 X 2 = 260
135	3	135 X 3 = 405
140	2	140 X 2 = 280
145	4	145 X 4 = 580
150	5	150 X 5 = 750
155	4	155 X 4 = 620
160	4	160 X 4 = 640
165	3	165 X 3 = 495
170	2	170 X 2 = 340
175	1	175 X 1 = 175
180	1	180 X 1 = 180
Totals	32	4,850

Explanation: Start by multiplying the height for each column by the number of pupils of that height (shown in the right-hand column). Then, add all those figures together to get 4,850. Then, divide 4,850 by 32 to get 151.5625. Round this up to 1 decimal place, giving you an answer of 151.6.

2.

Maths GCSE grades were recorded for 40 pupils. The data is shown on a cumulative frequency diagram below. Indicate all true statements below:

Maths GCSE grades recorded for 40 pupils

(1) 15 pupils get above Grade C. True or false?

True

(2) 30 pupils get above Grade D. True or false?

True

(3) 50% of the 40 pupils get a C Grade or above. True or false?

False

3.

A teacher represents the relationship between marks in a P.E test and an English test by the scatter graph shown below. The P.E marks are out of 20 and the English marks are out of 60. Indicate all true statements below:

(1) When the pupil's mark in P.E was 18, their English mark was also 18. True or false?

False

(2) The correlation between English and P.E marks in this test was positive. True or false?

True

(3) In general, if the mark in P.E was high, their mark in English was also high. True or false?

True

Numerical Reasoning

1. 12

Explanation: $\frac{3}{6} = \frac{1}{2}$. Half of the supervisors are male, which means that the other half are female. So, divide 24 by 2 to get 12.

2. 20

Explanation: Start by dividing 35 by 7 to get $\frac{1}{7}$ of 35 (5). Then, multiply 5 by 3 to get $\frac{3}{7}$ of 35 (15). Subtract 15 from 35 to get 20.

3. 9 hours and 18 minutes

Explanation: Start by adding 4 to 14 to get 18. Then, multiply 18 (the number of minutes spent on each exam paper) by 31 (the number of mock exams) to get 558 minutes. Divide 540 by 60 to get 9 hours, then add the remaining 18 minutes to get 9 hours and 18 minutes.

4. 7 hours

Explanation: Start by adding 9 to 3 to get 12. This is the amount of time spent marking each test. Then, multiply 12 by 35 to get 420, the total number of minutes spent marking all the tests. Divide 420 by 60 to get 7 hours.

5. 885 metres

Explanation: Divide 1,000 by 10 to get 10% of 1,000 (100). Multiply this by 8 to get 800. Then, divide 1,000 by 100 to get 1% of 1,000 (10). Multiply this by 8 to get 80. Then, divide 1,000 by 200 to get 0.5% of 1,000 (5). Then, add 800, 80 and 5 together to get 885 metres.

6. $\frac{17}{24}$

Explanation: Since these two fractions do not share the same denominator, they need to be changed. 24 is divisible by 8 and 12, so use that as the new denominator. Multiply $\frac{3}{8}$ by 3 to get $\frac{9}{24}$, and multiply $\frac{4}{12}$ by 2 to get $\frac{8}{24}$. Then, add 9 and 8 together to get $\frac{17}{24}$. This fraction cannot be simplified any further.

7. 10.25

Explanation: 100 minutes is the same as saying 1 hour and 40 minutes. Add 1 hour to 8.45, which then becomes 9.45. Then, add 40 minutes to 9.45 to get 10.25.

8. 9

Explanation: If there are 3 boys to every 4 girls per group, that means that there are 7 pupils per group (3 + 4 = 7). Divide 63 by 7 to get the number of groups needed: 9.

9. 75%

Explanation: Start by adding 86, 74 and 65 to get 225. Then, divide 225 by 3 to get 75%. Remember to include the percentage symbol in your answer.

INITIAL
TEACHER
TRAINING

Introduction

This chapter will discuss some of the details of teacher training, with the goal being to help you figure out for yourself whether becoming a teacher is the right path for you.

Before immersing yourself in teaching literature, you may have presupposed some things about the profession. You might have been tempted by the promise of long summer holidays or the fact that teaching is often described as "never boring". The aim of this chapter is to highlight facts about teaching, so that you know exactly what you're getting yourself into. This isn't to say that you should be deterred from teaching – it's fine to be incorrect about the details prior to becoming a teacher – but it is important that you know as much as possible about the profession before heading into it.

Almost all routes into teaching take *at least* one year to complete. This is the absolute minimum for becoming a teacher, and preparation might make the process even longer. For this reason, you need to be sure that teaching is for you. Sadly, you probably won't know for certain until you're actually in a classroom with a group of students. However, this chapter should help you get a better understanding of whether or not you want to become a teacher.

Routes into Teacher Training

As previously mentioned, there are a number of ways into the world of teaching. This section will outline some of the different opportunities for entering teacher training. Remember that all of these routes require you to have passed the QTS literacy and numeracy skills test.

PGCE

As the name suggests, the Postgraduate Certificate in Education (PGCE) is a postgraduate course taken after completing a degree. This is usually a good route to take if you have completed a degree in your preferred subject. For instance, perhaps you would like to become a history teacher. If you studied history at university, then taking a PGCE would allow you to become a history teacher. It isn't quite as rigid as this, however. In some cases, teachers may have specialised in one subject, such as history or geography, but perhaps moved into another related subject such as religious studies for teaching.

A full-time PGCE usually takes around nine months to complete, spending 24 weeks in a teaching environment. This will be separated over two separate key stages to give you broader experience teaching different age groups. Part-time PGCEs are also possible, but they will take longer to complete.

There are two main kinds of PGCE: school-led PGCEs which will see you in schools from the very beginning, and university-led PGCEs which will be more similar to a standard university degree. School-led PGCEs focus on observing experienced teachers in a real environment, whilst university-led PGCEs are taught in a university or college by lecturers and tutors.

PGCEs are led by different kinds of organisations. For example, some PGCEs may be run by Teach First, whilst others may be run by schools or other organisations. Essentially, the PGCE may be run in partnership with a variety of bodies, so it is important that you do some research on them as well. Some of these organisations will be discussed later in this chapter.

If you are currently a student at a university or college, or are on your way to studying for an undergraduate degree, more details can be found at events such as career fairs. These are a great opportunity to get even more specific information about PGCEs and speak face-to-face with a representative. Your university should have details about career fairs in their calendar.

In order to apply for a PGCE, you will need to meet the following requirements:

- GCSE grade C or higher in English and Maths;

- The pass mark in the QTS literacy and numeracy skills test (60% in literacy, 63% in numeracy);

- At least a 2:2 degree or its regional equivalent.

Depending on your situation, you may also need to meet the following:

- If English is not your first language and you don't have at least a C grade in GCSE English, you will need an IELTS with a score of at least 6.0;

- If you wish to teach pupils between the ages of 3 and 11, you will need at least a C grade in GCSE Science;

- If you want to teach in primary schools, a degree in a national curriculum subject is preferable;

- If you wish to teach in secondary schools, at least 50% of your degree must be in the subject which you are planning to teach.

On top of this, there are a few other requirements:

- A minimum of two weeks experience of working in a mainstream UK school. This experience needs to be recent;

- Medical fitness;

- A declaration of convictions from DBS.

Depending on your country of residence, the cost of tuition will vary:

- In 2016, the cost of tuition for a PGCE is £9,000 for UK and EU students;

- International students should expect to pay between £11,000 and £16,000.

Bear in mind that these figures are accurate as of 2016, and are subject to change.

A PGCE might not be for you. If this is the case, fear not – there are plenty of other routes into teaching which may suit your personal preferences, financial situation, and any other factors which may affect your choices. These will be covered in the rest of this chapter.

SCITT

School-Centred Initial Teacher Training (SCITT) involves trainees spending most of their time in schools. SCITT may be preferable to a PGCE for some because it allows you to select schools which are nearby. This means that you probably won't have to relocate.

Like a PGCE, SCITT trainees will have to teach in multiple schools. In addition, you will need to take short placements in other settings and educational venues. SCITT programmes are usually run by schools – sometimes groups of schools co-operate to run them.

The advantage of taking a SCITT course over a PGCE is that the training is incredibly practical. Most of the time is spent observing and learning from experienced teachers rather than lecturers or tutors. For some, this may be preferable to a university-led course.

Moreover, SCITT programmes are usually focused on local practices. This means that you will get experience in the local area, and probably learn some tips which are specific to it.

The requirements for SCITT are quite similar to those of a PGCE. You will need:

- An undergraduate degree;

- A grade C or higher in GCSE English and Maths;

- A grade C or higher in GCSE Science if you wish to teach pupils aged between 3 and 11;

- At least 60% in both the QTS literacy and numeracy tests.

If you have earned your qualifications outside of the UK, you must check to make sure that your grades are the equivalent of those required.

You will also need to meet the same extra-curricular requirements for PGCE: some recent classroom experience, medical fitness (which may involve a medical examination), a declaration of criminal convictions and a DBS check.

Applications for SCITT are made via UCAS.

School Direct (Salaried/Unsalaried)

School Direct is another route into teaching which focuses on learning while teaching, much like SCITT. School Direct comes in two different forms: salaried and unsalaried.

➢ School Direct (Salaried)

Trainees on the salaried version of School Direct will be employed by the school. While training, you will receive the salary of an unqualified teacher. The advantage of this is that you will be able to support yourself somewhat while training, and you will also receive practical teaching experience.

The requirements for School Direct are the same as those for SCITT. On top of that, you must be a graduate who has at least 3 years of experience in any career.

➢ School Direct (Unsalaried)

This version of School Direct is similar to its salaried counterpart, but as the name suggests, it will not be paid for by the school. You will not be paid a salary while taking this course, and will therefore need to pay for the tuition. However, you may be eligible for a student loan to complete your studies.

This route has the same requirements as the SCITT. Both the salaried and unsalaried versions of School Direct take around a year to complete.

Teach First

Teach First is a 2 year programme which has trainees working in schools which experience either poverty or under-achievement. In this programme, you will be employed as an unqualified teacher in a school. In your first year, you will complete a PGCE, whilst in the second year you will complete an NQT (Newly Qualified Teacher) induction.

Teach First might suit those who want experience in an environment which might be more challenging. Moreover, it's a great opportunity to help bring education to underprivileged pupils.

Teach First operates on a first come, first serve basis, and so it's important to get your application in as soon as possible.

How to start your application

Depending on which route you take, the application process will differ. In addition, different courses might be looking for slightly different qualities in candidates. Some routes may prefer candidates who are more practically-minded, whilst others may opt to recruit those with a more academic angle. Bear this in mind when writing your application, right up until after your interview. Hopefully you will have chosen a route which suits you best, making you a better fit, but keep an eye out for what these courses are looking for.

In this section, you will be given some general tips which will apply for any kind of teacher training application. Any differences between types of training will be noted where applicable.

For a UCAS application, you need to supply the following:

- **Your education history.** In particular, this section must include your GCSE and A-Level results, as well as your degree. This is to ensure that you meet the requirements for the training. This part of your application does not need intense detail – just list the qualifications you have obtained from school, college or university. If you are currently studying and do not have your results yet, you can list what grade(s) you are expected to receive.

- **Details regarding your highest qualification.** This is required because most teacher training courses require that the subject you wish to teach makes up at least 50% of your degree course. So, you will need to list all of the subjects or modules which made up your degree, as well as how much each was worth. This allows course recruiters to make sure your degree has covered enough of the subject.

- **QTS skills test information.** In this section, you will need to provide your registration number for the QTS skills tests, as well as the dates you took each test on.

- **Work experience/employment history.** This section requires that you discuss your work experience and employment history. You will have 500 characters to describe each job or part of work experience, so you will need to be concise. Make sure that you pick from a broad range of work experience if possible, and include the average time per week you spent at each. You can mention your employment history in your personal statement as well, but keep it brief and do not repeat the same information.

- **Your personal statement.** This is your opportunity to talk about yourself as a person, your experiences outside of work and education, and give the recruiters a taste of your personality. The personal statement will be discussed in more detail later in this chapter.

As with any application, clear and tidy presentation is vital to being a successful candidate. Teachers need to be organised, and need to be able to convey ideas in a concise manner. A muddled, clumsy application will demonstrate quite the opposite to an employer or recruiter. Here are some tips to help you make sure that your application is the best it can possibly be.

- **Take your time.** It will be obvious if your application is rushed. It will likely lack coherence, contain a number of grammatical or spelling errors and not represent you as well as possible. Teachers need to show that they are willing to put the time into their work, and the application process is a great way to showcase your ability to do so.

- **Proofread your work.** It is absolutely essential that your application is free from errors of any kind. With the knowledge obtained from the QTS literacy skills test, you are probably in a very good position to spot any errors in spelling, punctuation or grammar. Put these skills to use when writing your application, but make sure to be as thorough in your proofreading. This is a skill you will need as a teacher, either for marking work (applicable to some subjects), writing paperwork, or proofreading the work of a colleague.

Sometimes, we don't spot errors in our own work after reading and re-reading it constantly. In this case, it may be worth taking a break from your application, doing something else for a while, and then returning to read it again. New mistakes might reveal themselves after taking a break from proofreading. Ideally, you want a friend or relative proofreading your work as well, since they might spot things that you've glossed over. Additionally, having someone else proofread your application will demonstrate whether what you've written is clear and easy to understand. You know what you mean when you write the application, but someone who isn't you might struggle to understand what you've written. Therefore, it is incredibly useful to have a second opinion when proofreading your application.

- **Keep it tidy.** Most teacher training applications are now done online, which means that you don't have to worry about your handwriting for the time being. However, you should make sure that your style is consistent in the application. If you apply by uploading a document with your application attached, make sure that you've used the same font and font size consistently throughout. Also make sure that the font you use is appropriate – nothing unprofessional, and certainly nothing that is barely legible.

By following these tips, you should have an application that looks great and reads well. Now, all you need to know is exactly what to include.

- **Only include relevant information.** While style and presentation is incredibly important, substance is paramount. By making sure that you include all of the relevant details (and omit irrelevant information), you are clearly presenting your finest qualities. You won't have a lot of space to write everything, so you need to get to the point and avoid waffling.

The Personal Statement

When applying for teacher training, you will have to write a personal statement. Essentially, this is a short piece of writing which you can use to sell yourself as a candidate. In this section, you will learn what recruiters like to see in a personal statement.

- **Demonstrate your passion for teaching.** Recruiters and employers need to know that you're passionate. If you come across as bored or unenthusiastic, you're unlikely to be chosen for the role. No matter how passionate you are, it's entirely possible for this to not come across in writing. So make sure that you express your desire to become a teacher in a mature and focused way. It may help to explain your motive for wanting to become a teacher, as well. Perhaps you had an excellent teacher at school who inspired you, or maybe you're simply enthusiastic about imparting knowledge onto others. Whatever the case may be, try and get this across. However, make sure you don't devote too much space to this in your statement – you want to remain concise.

- **Include some relevant experience.** Outside of your mandatory experience in a school, do you have any experience which may strengthen your application? Perhaps you've done volunteering in an underprivileged area, or have some experience in public speaking. Any experiences which convey desirable qualities for a teacher should be included. Briefly explain what this experience was and how it relates to teaching. So, public speaking experience might have made you a more confident speaker, which might be useful in a classroom. Volunteering in the local area might have made you more aware of social issues which could help you empathise with some pupils. By linking your experiences to teaching, you can make yourself look like a strong candidate.

- **Briefly discuss relevant part-time and other work experience.** If you don't have much unpaid experience, it may be worth referring to your work experience in order to strengthen your application. You don't need to go into great detail about every job you've had – your employment history will be covered outside of the personal statement – but any activities during your employment which may sell you as a candidate can be used in your personal statement.

- **Present yourself.** Your personal statement is a chance to show who you are as a person, and there are a number of ways in which you can demonstrate your personality. In many cases, it is better to show who you are through experiences, hobbies and any other activities rather than just writing your qualities out. Lots of volunteering may show compassion or commitment, whilst demonstrating sportiness through completion of marathons or other activities might show determination. It's worth remembering that, in your personal statement, almost every piece of information you give should reflect on you. Demonstrate how your past work experience, volunteering and hobbies have shaped you as a person and made you into the perfect candidate for the role.

Following these tips will strengthen your application, hopefully to the point where you are offered an interview. In the next section, you will learn what to do before, during and after your interview to maximise your chance of being a successful candidate.

How to prepare for the interview

So far, your application will have given the employer or recruiter some idea of who you are, what your strengths are, and what experiences you've had. However, an interview is an opportunity for them to get to know you in person and double-check any information you've provided in the application form.

The interview is also used to gauge your interest in teaching. If you're enthusiastic about becoming a teacher, that should come across quite naturally in the interview. To help you, here are some general tips for coming across as an ideal candidate during the interview.

- Presentation matters. Just as you'd make your application look neat, tidy and concise, it is important that you adjust your appearance for the interview. From an appearance perspective, treat the teacher training interview like any other. Dress smart and adopt an appropriate posture.

- Take notes. You should bring some pens and paper in order to take some notes during the interview. Writing notes allows you to raise any questions at the end of the interview, in case anything is unclear. It also shows that you have a genuine interest in teaching and the training, since you're making the effort to listen carefully and take note of anything that might be particularly important. Moreover, bringing note paper gives you the opportunity to prepare some questions beforehand and then ask them at the end of the interview. You needn't go overboard and ask too many questions, but it never hurts to express a few sensible queries so long as there's time.

- Be prepared. Before entering your interview, make sure you know what you're going to be asked. For example, the interviewers won't ask about your own political views, but knowledge about current political affairs shows an awareness of prevalent issues. In particular, keep a close eye on any changes in policy which may affect teaching. You could be asked to discuss an issue which has an impact on teaching, and so it is helpful to know a bit about the current political landscape before offering your opinion.

The interviewers don't expect you to know all the details of teaching. After all, you're there for the opportunity to learn more about teaching, and so the interviewers won't mind too much if you aren't clear on every precise detail. If you intend become a secondary school teacher, it's possible that the interviewers will ask questions about the subject you wish to teach. You probably won't get asked too much about what you studied at degree level, so take time to find out what pupils learn in your subject while at school. The curriculum may have changed significantly since you were at school, so conduct some research on what pupils learn currently in order to answer questions accurately.

Remember that the interviewers may ask you about anything in your application, including your personal statement. When preparing for the interview, revisit your application to remember what you wrote about your employment experiences, and the details of your personal statement. Be ready to expand on the points you make, possibly giving more evidence as to why you'd make a great student and teacher.

Ultimately, you need to be able to show enthusiasm for teaching at all times. The best way to do this is to know your stuff and show that you are interested in teaching. The fact that you have taken the time to learn information about the course and teaching in general shows that you are keen, so what you need to do is gear your answers to demonstrate this further. However, don't come across as so enthusiastic that you haven't considered the fine details. Enthusiasm is key, but it's also vital to come across as calm and collected. Try to strike the balance between the two.

In the next section, you will learn some general tips on how to come across as an excellent candidate in your application and interview.

A guide to being an excellent candidate

The focus of this section is to give some tips on what makes a great candidate. These tips will apply to your application and interview, as well as giving some general ideas for teaching as a whole.

- **Balance is key.** It's often said that teachers need to be thick-skinned in order to deal with their environment. This is only partly true. It's certainly the case that a teacher cannot be too sensitive: they need to be able to deal with students who might cause trouble or perhaps even offense. More often than not, these pupils do not mean what they say, and therefore you need to bear this in mind and be resilient in some situations.

However, you cannot completely block out criticism. You need to be able to listen to genuine concerns from colleagues and students, which means that that you can't ignore everything that is said to you. For example, a pupil may complain rather obnoxiously that you're moving through the material at too fast a pace, making it difficult for them to keep up. While they may have been rude in expressing their opinion, and you might want to simply block it out and continue as normal, it is important that you take the criticism on-board.

The most effective teachers will strike a balance between blocking out useless criticism/complaints and being mindful of genuine issues raised by pupils and colleagues. It's vital that a teacher is thick-skinned to an extent, but not so much that they become oblivious to real problems.

- **Be willing to learn.** Even though you are training to become a teacher, it doesn't mean that your learning days are over. You need to show an openness to new ideas in teaching, as well as be prepared to be wrong about a few things. Since you're applying for teacher training, you're probably aware of this, but this is a quality that you need to somehow demonstrate in your application. Stubbornness won't go too far in the world of teaching, and you need to be ready to adopt new ideas - from the day you start training, until the day that you retire from teaching.

In your application, it may be worth giving some experience which shows that you are willing to learn. Perhaps you've received additional non-compulsory training while in the workplace, or you've attended talks in your spare time. Either way, it is important that you draw some attention to this in your application and interview. Being enthusiastic about jumping into teaching is important, but you also need to demonstrate that you are willing to learn.

A willingness to learn is a quality that needs to be maintained throughout your career as a teacher, and ties into the earlier point about being sensitive to criticism. Not only are you going to have colleagues and students making observations about your teaching style and ways to improve, but new ways of teaching effectively are being introduced quite regularly. You need to be ready to take on new ideas in order to be an excellent teacher.

- Be confident. If you pass the application and interview process, it's clear that the tutors, recruiters or employers who have picked you believe that you are capable of becoming a teacher. Even if you've only made it to the interview, you've clearly done enough to impress the recruiters somewhat – they just want some kind of verification of your qualities. Since you've already made it this far, you can feed confident in your ability.

Teachers need to be confident in order to perform well in schools, and confidence while training will help you make the most out of the process. In a teaching environment, a lack of confidence will show as you are less committed to your actions, which could result in underperformance. Of course, you don't want to be over-confident or arrogant since these traits can be difficult for others to deal with, making it more difficult for colleagues to deal with you in the process. Likewise, you can't act as if you know it all, because you almost certainly don't – there's always more to learn.

Conclusion

Becoming a teacher isn't a simple process, but hopefully this chapter has revealed the routes into teacher training for you. Additionally, the information given should give you an idea of what to write in your application, what to say in the interview, and how to generally behave in both – as well as in the training and teaching environments.

A FEW FINAL WORDS...

You have reached the end of your guide to passing the QTS skills tests and making your way into teacher training. If you have read the information in this book, attempted the mock tests, and read through the tips provided, you should be on your way to passing the real thing. Hopefully, you will feel far more confident in what you know as well as what you need to improve.

For any test or training, it is helpful to consider the following…

The Three P's

1. **Preparation.** Preparation is key to passing any psychometric test; you won't be doing yourself any favours by not taking the time to prepare. Many fail their tests because they did not know what to expect or did not know what their own weaknesses were. Take the time to re-read any areas you may have struggled with, and take another look at the sample questions before attempting the real test. By doing this, you will become familiar with how you will perform on the day of the test.

2. **Perseverance.** If you set your sights on a goal and stick to it, you are more likely to succeed. Obstacles and setbacks are common when trying to achieve something great, and you shouldn't shy away from them. Instead, face the tougher parts of the test, even if you feel defeated. If you need to, take a break from your work to relax and then return with renewed vigour. If you fail the test, take the time to consider why you failed, gather your strength and try again.

3. **Performance.** How well you perform will be the result of your preparation and perseverance. Remember to relax when taking the test and try not to panic. Believe in your own abilities, practice as much as you can, and motivate yourself constantly. Nothing is gained without hard work and determination, and this applies to how you perform on the day of the test.

Good luck with your QTS skills tests and teacher training. We wish you the best of luck with all of your future endeavours!

The how2become team

The How2Become Team

Glossary

WORD/PHRASE	DEFINITION
Adjective	A word used to describe a noun. Can be shortened to 'adj'. Examples: 'long', 'tough', 'extraordinary', 'broken'.
Adverb	A word used to modify a verb. Bears a similar relationship with verbs as adjectives and nouns do. Adverbs describe the way in which the verb is occurring. Examples: 'gently', 'slowly', 'fast', 'approvingly'.
Capital Letter	An upper case version of a letter (R, L, P etc.), used for the first letter of every sentence and for proper nouns (see noun).
Clause	A unit of measurement for a collection of words. Smaller than a sentence, and must contain a subject and a verb.
Cohesive Device/ Sentence Adverb	A word or phrase used to connect two sentences in a particular way. Depending on the relationship between the sentences, different cohesive devices are appropriate. Examples: 'however', 'furthermore', 'therefore', 'in addition'.

Colon (:)	A punctuation mark used to introduce a list or add further explanation to a clause.
Comma (,)	A punctuation mark used to separate clauses and items in lists. It often shows the reader that there is meant to be a pause in reading that isn't as strong as a full stop.
Comparative	A kind of adjective or adverb which compares two things. Examples: 'better', 'happier', 'stronger'.
Consonant	A series of statements which oppose one another or say two different things which cannot both be the case.
Dash (–)	A punctuation mark used to show a break in a sentence for additional information. It is stronger than a comma. Not to be confused with a hyphen, which is shorter.
Determiner	A word used to modify a noun or group noun. Determiners usually denote the quantity of the noun. Examples: 'every', 'a', 'the'.
Ellipsis (…)	A punctuation mark used to create tension or leave a sentence hanging. It can also show where a quotation has been shortened to only include the relevant parts.

Exclamation Mark (!)	A punctuation mark to show statements which are forceful or surprising. It is often used in dialogue to signify a raised voice. Like full stops, exclamation marks show the end of a sentence.
Full Stop (.)	A punctuation mark used to show the end of a sentence.
Homophone	A set of two or more words which sound the same when spoken, but are spelled differently and have different meanings. Examples: 'air/heir', 'to/two/too' 'there/their'.
Hyphen (-)	A punctuation mark used to show where two words have been combined to create a compound word. Not to be confused with a dash, which is longer. Examples of compound words: 'light-hearted', 're-election'.
Implication	A conclusion which can be drawn from a statement, although it is not explicit. Usually passive: a text will imply something.
Inference	Like implication, an inference is a conclusion drawn from a statement. Unlike implication, a subject infers something from a text or statement.

Noun	A word used to identify objects, people, animals or places. These come in two forms: proper nouns and common (or improper) nouns. Proper nouns include the names of people and places. Proper nouns are always capitalised, whilst improper nouns are not capitalised.
	Examples of proper nouns:
	'John', 'Mexico', 'Katie'.
	Examples of improper nouns:
	'cat', 'airport', 'man', 'woman'.
Paragraph	A way of breaking up a text into smaller parts. A paragraph is made up of sentences, and usually covers one key topic.
Parentheses ()	Also known as brackets, parentheses are used to add extra information to a text as an aside.
Participle	A word which is a modified verb acting as an adjective or a noun.
	Examples of participles:
	'working man', 'speeding car'.
Prefix	A word or letter placed at the beginning of a word to change its meaning. In many cases, a prefix changes the meaning of the word to its opposite (e.g. 'appropriate' and 'inappropriate')
	Examples of prefixes:
	'im-', 'in-' 'un-'

Preposition	A word or phrase used to describe where a noun is in time and space. Examples: 'on', 'in', 'beside', 'during', 'until'.
Pronoun	A word which acts as a substitute for a noun. Depending on the subjects and tenses, different pronouns will be appropriate. Examples: 'he', 'she', 'they', 'I', 'you', 'himself', 'herself'.
Question Mark (?)	A punctuation mark which signifies a question. Question marks end a sentence in the same way that a full stop does.
Quotation Mark (')	A punctuation mark which appears in a pair. This indicates words which are not those of the narrator or writer, such as speech or a quotation from another source. A quotation mark appears at the beginning of the quote and also at the end.
Semicolon (;)	A punctuation mark used to separate major parts of a sentence. Usually, the semicolon can join two pieces of text which are related but could stand on their own as two separate sentences.
Sentence Fragment	A grammatical error in which a piece of writing is closed off with a full stop, but does not form a proper sentence.
Speech Mark ("")	A punctuation mark used to show speech, usually in the form of dialogue. These are often used interchangeably with quotation marks. Like quotation marks, they always come in pairs: once at the start of the speech and once at the end.

Subject	A person or other kind of thing (e.g. animals) that is being discussed in the sentence. Each sentence requires at least one subject.
Subordinate Clause	A secondary clause which is dependent on the main clause of the sentence in order to make sense.
Suffix	A collection of letters added to the end of a word to change its meaning. Examples: '-ly', '-ation', '-ing'.
Superlative	An adjective or adverb which signifies something being of the highest degree in a certain quality. Examples: 'strongest', 'largest', 'calmest'.
Syllable	A measurement of text which is smaller than a word. A word is made of one or more syllables.
Synonym	A word or phrase which means the same thing as another word. Examples: 'anxious/nervous', 'intimidate/scare'.
Tautology	An error which occurs when the same thing is said twice but with different words. This is also referred to as a redundancy. Examples of tautologous phrases: 'suddenly exploded', 'written down', '9am in the morning'.

Tense	A modification of a word in order to demonstrate its place in time (past/present/future). Depending on the tense of the sentence or phrase, a different word is necessary.
Tone	Tone describes the general attitude of a piece of writing or other material. This includes serious, light-hearted, formal and informal.
Verb	A word used to describe state or action. These are sometimes referred to as 'doing' words. A sentence requires at least one verb as well as one subject in order to be a proper sentence. Examples: 'run', 'jump', 'write', 'read'.
Vowel	There are five vowels in the English alphabet – a, e, i, o, u. These combine with consonants in order to form syllables and words.

Check out our QTS Professional Skills Test Books

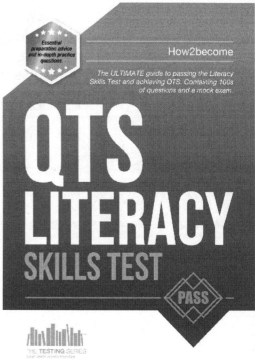

FOR MORE INFORMATION ON OUR QTS SKILLS TEST GUIDES, PLEASE CHECK OUT THE FOLLOWING:

WWW.HOW2BECOME.COM

NEED FURTHER GUIDANCE? CHECK OUT OUR TEACHER TRAINING RESOURCES

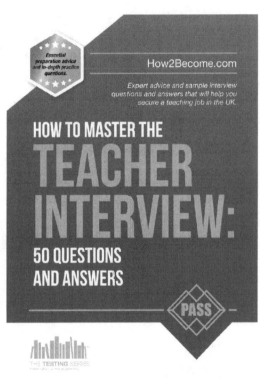

FOR MORE INFORMATION ON OUR QTS SKILLS TEST GUIDES, PLEASE CHECK OUT THE FOLLOWING:

WWW.HOW2BECOME.COM